Listening Hearts

Discerning Call in Community

Listening

Morehouse Publishing
NEW YORK

Suzanne G. Farnham
Joseph P. Gill
R. Taylor McLean
Susan M. Ward

Hearts

Discerning Call in Community

With New and Updated Content
Foreword by Eugene Taylor Sutton

30TH ANNIVERSARY EDITION

Morehouse Publishing, 19 East 34th Street,
New York, NY 10016
Morehouse Publishing is an imprint of
Church Publishing Incorporated.
www.churchpublishing.org

A record of this book is available from the Library of Congress.

ISBN: 978-1-64065-413-6 (paperback)
ISBN: 978-1-64065-414-3 (ebook)

To Jenifer Ballard Ramberg, our friend and co-worker, who experienced her own personal struggle with hearing God's call. Her unique contributions came from her knowledge of feminist theology, and she guided and prodded us in the early stages of this book's development. Her untimely death is felt deeply by each of us individually, and our working group has sorely missed her.

Contents

Acknowledgments

The authors are grateful for the assistance and support provided to us in writing this 30th Anniversary Edition. Stephanie Hull, Patty McLean, Frances Sullinger, and Norma Williamson worked extensively to help update the appendices. The Rev. Tim Grayson contributed to the updated annotated bibliography. Laura McConnell, office manager for Listening Hearts Ministries, cheerfully assisted us as needed. The Rt. Rev. Eugene Taylor Sutton graciously wrote the foreword. Church Publishing initiated this opportunity to update our work and publish it in Spanish, with a special thanks to our editor Nancy Bryan.

Thirty years is a blink of an eye and an eternity. The authors are grateful for the opportunity to work together again.

For all that has been, Thanks.
For all that will be, Yes.[1]

Foreword to the 30th Anniversary Edition of Listening Hearts

I first met Suzanne Farnham in the spring of 2001 at Washington National Cathedral, where I was serving as the cathedral's canon for spiritual formation and director of the Cathedral Center for Prayer and Pilgrimage. Those were the years of the Cathedral sponsoring large conferences with thousands of people hearing dozens of famous speakers, but the prayer center itself was holding smaller gatherings at the time specifically for refugees from normal church life—labyrinth walkers, meditators, contemplative practitioners, Christian spiritual nomads, and other seekers—who wanted to deepen their relationship with God and others in an authentic spiritual community.

Two books were handed to me that Suzanne co-wrote with others in her learning community: *Listening Hearts: Discerning Call in Community* and *Grounded in God: Listening Hearts Discernment for Group Deliberations*. The first volume was a primer for how someone can discern God's call in the context of a listening community, and the second was a guide for decision-making groups on how to incorporate practical spirituality and consensus-building into their meetings. I was more than excited to read these books, which I devoured immediately, and have since come back to again and again for the spiritual wisdom contained in them. I invited Suzanne to come to the Cathedral as part of our Lenten series on spiritual practices to introduce her guidelines for discernment before a rather surprisingly large group of attendees. We were especially eager to hear her insights into how we could use Listening Hearts principles to create small prayer groups within the cathedral community.

Not long after that wonderful evening, the Center for Prayer and Pilgrimage launched several weekly gatherings for centering prayer, scripture meditation, spiritual direction, and other ancient spiritual practices that have lain dormant in much of the church for centuries. At these small gatherings in some simple prayer rooms in a large gothic-style cathedral, we learned to listen to one another's stories. And we learned to listen to God.

Listening is the bedrock discipline of the spiritual life. Many, of course, would insist that prayer itself is the primary discipline, but what is prayer except a journey into mutual listening? Mother Teresa was once asked what she says to God when she prays. She replied:

> "I don't say anything. I just listen." The questioner persisted, "Well then, what does God say to you?" "He doesn't say anything. He just listens."

I have been listening to God ever more deeply because of Listening Hearts Ministries, which Suzanne founded in 1987. It began as a grassroots effort in Baltimore among several communities of faith to help people understand the dynamics of discerning God's call to them in their personal relationships, vocational choices, ordering of priorities, and responses to moral or ethical dilemmas. Through workshops, conferences, and individual consultations, Listening Hearts has been a faithful guide to thousands of people who make the journey into spiritual discernment. I have benefitted personally from meeting regularly with Suzanne and a few other Spirit guides ever since I became a bishop in 2008; it is through these monthly spiritual discernment sessions that I have been sustained in my vocation as well as in all other aspects of my life. We are grounded in the principles contained in this newly revised version of *Listening Hearts*.

This thirtieth anniversary edition of what is destined to become a classic spiritual work is needed now more than ever. We live in uncertain times, and our society's need for more spiritual grounding is palpable; this book is well positioned to meet that need. The new edition also recognizes the changing twenty-first-century religious landscape. Reflecting the growing diversity of faith expressions, it has been updated to invite more seekers who claim to be "spiritual but not religious." There is no better time than now to reach out to persons who do not darken the doors of our houses of worship.

The spiritual writer and retreat leader Sister Joyce Rupp, OSM, reflecting on what the future may hold for us both as individuals and as a society, once said:

> When the time is ripe,
>   the vision will come.
> When the heart is ready,
>   the fruit will appear.
> When the soul is mature.
>   the harvest will happen.

The time is ripe. Our hearts are ready. The soul of *Listening Hearts* has matured.

The harvest will happen.

The Rt. Rev. Eugene Taylor Sutton
Bishop, Episcopal Diocese of Maryland
March 3, 2021

Foreword to 20th Anniversary Edition of Listening Hearts

I met Suzanne Farnham in April of 1987 at a retreat I co-led with Walter and June Wink at Kirkridge. I was grateful for the quality of her presence and participation, and I was glad to see her again at another conference in the early 1990s. I *thought* I remembered her well. But the accuracy of my memory was called into serious doubt when Suzanne spoke to the group and said, "Parker Palmer is the father of my child."

That part of our Kirkridge experience I did *not* remember. Nor do I remember what I said, if anything, after Suzanne's comment got everyone's attention, including mine. But I was relieved when she explained, amid much laughter, that her "child" was the 1991 book *Listening Hearts* (co-authored with Joseph Gill, R. Taylor McLean, and Susan Ward) which had been inspired, in part, by elements of the Kirkridge retreat.

For a twenty-year-old, this book has served so many people so well that I am proud to claim a very minor role in its lineage. I am also grateful for a chance to say a few words about it, because *Listening Hearts* focuses on a question that has been very close to my heart for a long time: How can we listen for our vocation, for God's calling in our lives, and listen for it in community, in the Body of Christ?

In my mid-thirties, at a time when my own calling was a source of great confusion to me, I was attracted to Quakerism. My attraction had much to do with the twin pillars of Quaker spirituality as I understand it: the conviction that every human being has direct inward access to God, and the equally strong conviction that we need a community of discernment to help us sort and sift what we *think* we are hearing from within. As depth psychology and good theology remind us—and as many of us know from experience—not every voice from within is the voice of God. It is easy to find examples of people who have mistaken the voice of ego or some deeper darkness for the voice of truth, following it down a path of personal ruination, sometimes taking others with them.

So listening for one's calling is tricky business. From personal experience I know that one's hearing can be blocked by a wide range of inner dynamics, from thinking too poorly of yourself to thinking too highly of yourself. If I suffer from ego inflation, I am likely to have grandiose visions of what I can do in the world, leading me into activities that will damage me or others. If I suffer from ego deflation, I am likely to shy away from an important calling that will stretch me but that I have the gifts to pursue.

In *Let Your Life Speak*, I tell about a moment when I felt sure that becoming the president of a small educational institution was the thing for me. I took my—well, my ego—to a Clearness Committee, a Quaker discernment process mentioned in *Listening Hearts*. About an hour into the process (after I had answered many questions about my calling with a certainty which had begun to feel not exactly God-given), someone asked me a simple question: "What would you like most about being president?"

I thought for a while, decided it was time to get honest, then started listing things I would *not* like. My list was long, ranging from how I would have to dress, to being on call all the time, to my intense dislike of faculty politics. My questioner gently reminded me that the question was about what I would *like*. I thought some more and—having tired of answering questions from my ego rather than my heart—I finally said, sheepishly, "I guess the only thing I'd really like is seeing my picture in the paper with the word 'president' under it."

After a studied silence in which I had to stew in my own answer, my questioner spoke again: "Parker, can you think of an easier way to get your picture in the paper?"

That story makes me laugh, of course, at myself. But it also evokes my gratitude. As a person who lacks some of the key gifts necessary for institutional leadership, the decision I made to turn down that presidency and keep seeking my true calling saved me—and the educational institution in question—from a sad fate. I am deeply grateful for the way a true community of discernment can help us sift and winnow the many messages we get from inside and outside of ourselves, separating the wheat from the chaff.

Creating and holding a space for discernment is profoundly counter-cultural work. We live in a culture that too often regards us as empty vessels to be filled with someone else's knowledge, someone else's agenda, someone else's truth—and churches can be among the worst offenders in this regard. Spiritual discernment is not about telling each other what to do. Spiritual discernment is about trusting the fact that all of us are made in God's image and all of us have access to God's call for our lives. It is about practicing the disciplines required to help ourselves and each other heal the internal wounds and surmount the external obstacles that keep us from hearing that call.

Listening Hearts is a book that has helped tens of thousands of people in the churches do exactly that. I cannot lay claim to being its proud father. But as a more distant relative, I commend this book to you, doing so with enthusiasm and gratitude as it enters its third decade of service.

Parker J. Palmer
Author of *A Hidden Wholeness*,
Let Your Life Speak, and
The Courage to Teach
October 2010

Listening Hearts

Discerning Call in Community

Introduction

"Be patient toward all that is unsolved in your heart and try to love the *questions themselves*," wrote the poet Rainer Maria Rilke.[1] The questions of our time—myriad, persistent, and often vexing—are not new. Human beings have always struggled to understand the meaning of who they are and how to find their true path and follow it. In 1835, Soren Kierkegaard wrote in his journal:

> What I really lack is to be clear in my mind *what I am to do*, *not* what am I to know. . . . The thing is to understand myself, to see what God really wishes *me* to do.[2]

This book is about discerning God's call in community, a call that comes in various ways, to people of faith and to seekers of truth who may be spiritual, but not religious. Though written from a Judeo-Christian background, the principles that underlie this book—informed and enriched by other traditions—are universal in nature.

First published in 1991, the nine chapters of *Listening Hearts* draw from classical literature to present the complexities of spiritual discernment in clear, concise language that is easy to understand. The 30th Anniversary Edition updates these chapters to refine the wording to reflect the passage of time and expand the language for a wider audience. It adds a section of "Stories of Call" that come from individual real-life experiences and revises the Appendices of Practical Suggestions that help people cultivate a life of discernment. This edition also updates the annotated bibliography to include some books that have expanded our understanding of call over the intervening years. Among these are works about how science and history inform religion and spirituality—including the concept that the universe both influences and responds to our interactions with it.[3]

Before the authors began their work thirty years ago, a group of forty people studied writers who, over the centuries, had explored questions of call, discernment, and community. Using a color-coded system, the readers underlined and highlighted passages in the books to indicate information relating to these topics. The authors met weekly for two years, reviewing the material and writing the book, using the model of the Quakers: beginning and ending in silence, listening to one another prayerfully, and waiting for consensus to emerge. Every sentence in the book reflects this approach.

This book can be used for meditation. If a sentence or phrase gives pause, it can be fruitful to stop, hold it in silence, then reflect on it. It may point to a place where God touches your life. Additionally, this book can be a springboard for group sharing. By reading a designated chapter in advance and marking portions that particularly speak to them—or that they do not fully grasp—participants pave the way for conversation that arises from their own experience.

Appendices provide guidelines for a small group to gather in prayer and reflectively pose questions to help an individual find clarity around an issue of personal concern. Notes that credit sources and delve beneath the surface of concepts put forth in the book appear at the end so as not to interfere with the flow of the text.

The heart is the hub of all sacred spaces.
Go there and roam.[4]

Call

ONE

What Is "Call"?

. . . let each of you lead the life . . . to which God called you.
–1 Cor. 7:17

People call us to get our attention, to make contact with us, to draw us closer to them. So it is with God. A call may come as a gradual dawning of purpose for our lives. It can involve an accelerating sense of inner direction. It can emerge through a gnawing feeling that we need to do a specific thing. On occasion, it can burst forth as a sudden awareness of a path that God would have us take. Call may be emphatic and unmistakable, or it may be obscure and subtle.[1] In whatever way call is experienced, through the centuries God has chosen to speak to us and bids us to listen. "I will instruct you and teach you the way you should go; I will counsel you with my eye upon you" (Ps. 32:8).

God calls us on many levels: God calls creation, calls the Church, calls my congregation, and calls me, today, to reach me where I am now. God calls the entirety of my life. And at specific times and places, God calls me to particular actions.

God calls each of us. There are a variety of calls, and no one call is inherently better or higher than any other. The call of a priest, monk, or nun, however sacred, is not superior in and of itself to the call of an architect, a mechanic, or a nurse.[2] It is our faithfulness to God and not our station in life that honors a call.[3]

We need to look beneath external facts to determine a call. For example, two men might be wrestling with what seems to be the same question: whether or not to volunteer at a breakfast program for homeless people. For one, the call might turn out to be to stay home and spend some much-needed time with his children. For the other, the call might be to work at the breakfast program and help his family develop a sense of supporting him in service to others.

God speaks to us through the language of everyday events.[4] Each new moment of life, each new situation, the present condition of a person or community, of events, time, place, people, and circumstances—all hold clues to God's call.[5] Thus, we often find our calls in the facts, circumstances, and concrete experiences of daily life.[6]

Sometimes call comes through what is imposed on us. Teresa of Avila, for instance, wrote several books because her confessors told her to. Today, with hindsight, we can recognize that through her obedience she was honoring God's call. Similarly, Dietrich Bonhoeffer found in prison a call to minister to others who were imprisoned.

Any matter, large or small, may relate to our call. A call could encompass a decision about whether to take a new job, go back to school, volunteer at a shelter. A call could draw us to a personal relationship in a new or different way. A call could focus on whether to resist paying taxes as a form of protest or whether to sell all our belongings and move to another country. A call may not be so much a call to "do" as to "be." An active man may become sick and unable to do what he has done before; yet while he may not be called to be sick, he may be called in sickness to reflect God's presence and love in a new way. So call should be understood in the widest, most inclusive sense, to encompass what we do and who we are.

This is not to say that in every decision there is a call from God or that God is always giving us guidance regarding every question we face. Sometimes we need to act based upon our assessment of what is good—we need to make a decision. In such a situation, elevating the decision to a call from God will not make it one.[7]

On the other hand, because a matter seems unimportant does not foreclose a call from God. As with God's call to Moses, the desire to minister at a soup kitchen or as a school volunteer can burn brightly with the fire of God's call.

A call might lead us to pursue a certain occupation or career, as a person who feels called to help others in turmoil might become a pastoral counselor. Quite often a call becomes visible in a specific job, task, or endeavor. But a call can never be reduced to such activities. The same counselor may also be called to care for family, friends, and community as well as clients and thus must balance all of these in order to be faithful to the call. In a world that puts much emphasis on success, a too-narrow concern with occupation or career can make us deaf to our calls.[8]

We may be called beyond ordinary occupations—to be prophets. A prophet does not have to be a Moses or a Jeremiah. Amos, for example, was a shepherd who left his flock to become a prophet in Israel, returning home when his years of prophesying came to an end. So, too, any one of us may be called to a prophetic role at a specific time and place for a specific issue.

Not only is every call unique, but the hearing of every call is unique also. One sign that God may be calling is a certain restlessness, a certain dissatisfaction with things as they are. Other signs of call may be a sense of longing, yearning, or wondering; a feeling of being at a crossroads; a sense that something is happening in one's life, that one is wrestling with an issue or decision; a sense of being in a time of transition; or a series of circumstances that draw one into a specific issue.

While role models are helpful, we are not called to copy other people.[9] Rather, we are to become fully the people God created us to be, living our own lives in response to our own calls—as Jesus lived out his life faithful to God's call for him.[10] So it is that hearing one's call is akin to discovering one's own self.[11]

Even when a need exists and we are well qualified to meet it, we are not necessarily called to respond to it. Something may seem logical for us to do, but that does not mean that God calls us to do it. In ordinary circumstances, people analyze facts in order to come to a conclusion. While this is a useful exercise, it is not the same thing as discerning God's call.

> This is the irrational season
> When love blooms bright and wild.
> Had Mary been filled with reason
> There'd have been no room for the child.[12]

Ultimately, it is not what the evidence suggests but the source of the call that gives it authority.

Similarly, simply because a task or undertaking is good to do does not mean that we are called to do it or that we should continue doing it. To be doing what is good can be the greatest obstacle to doing something even better.[13] We may understand only with hindsight why we were called to do something different.

Call usually involves service or benefit to others. In fact, a sense of call may be suspect if it does not involve service.[14] Nonetheless, the fruits of call are sometimes a long time in coming;[15] indeed, we may never perceive them. Things we say or do can have a profound impact we may never know about. Sometimes the fruits of our life manifest themselves at a much later time, perhaps even after our death.[16] The Letter to the Hebrews reminds us of this in its account of Abraham and Sarah:

> By faith Abraham obeyed when he was called to set out for a place that he was to receive as an inheritance; and he set out, not knowing where he was going. By faith he stayed for a time in the Land he had been promised. . . . By faith he received power of procreation, even though he was too old—and Sarah herself was barren—because he considered him faithful who had promised.
>
> All of these died in faith without having received the promises, but from a distance they saw and greeted them. (Heb. 11:8, 9, 11, 13)

Every true call is a call to obey God; indeed, the word *obedience* derives from the Latin *audire*, which means "to listen."[17] Jesus came to include us in his divine obedience,[18] saying, "If you love me, you will keep my commandments" (John 14:15), and "They who have my commandments and keep them are those who love me . . ." (John 14:21). If we love God, we want to live in harmony with God—we want to hear what God has to say, and we want to act on what we hear. St. Paul refers to this as "obedient from the heart" (Rom. 6:17).

While call requires response and obedience, we will not be given a road map. Our response to a call is not mechanical application. Rather, call requires that we take responsibility. We will not necessarily be called to come up with a correct answer, as in a crossword puzzle, but something freer and more creative. We are given building blocks to see what can be done with them, using for the task all of our intelligence, creativity, sensitivity, and love. Our critical faculties are required; we must use them the best way we can, constructively and with love.[19]

Awareness of a call may give rise to a feeling of inadequacy, as illustrated in the classical biblical calls of Moses, Jeremiah, and Isaiah. Moses said no five times to God (Exod. 3:11, 13; 4:1, 10, 13). Moses' excuses included not knowing God's name, not being a person of consequence, not having credibility, and not being a good speaker. Jeremiah responded to God, "Ah, Lord God! Truly I do not know how to speak, for I am only a boy" (Jer. 1:6). Before Isaiah could say, "Here I am," in response to God's call, he expressed his profound sense of unworthiness with the cry, "I am a man of unclean lips" (Isa. 6:5).

Yet God not only calls but empowers—although the power may come only as we respond. Conversely, if we don't respond to a call, we may become increasingly blind and deaf to God's promptings. To ignore or resist a call may "fracture us further, widening the split between what we subscribe to inwardly and what we do outwardly."[20]

Our calls are always evolving. If we are to respond, we need to listen, not only today but as today evolves into tomorrow. In times of transition, we need to listen with extra care. "If we go on listening, we feel God pulling us, drawing us into another current, a larger, deeper, stronger one than our usual little force."[21]

Morning by morning he wakens—
wakens my ear
to listen as those who are taught.
The Lord God has opened my ear. . . .
-Isa. 50:4–5

TWO

Call to Ministry

Jesus said to them . . . "As the Father has sent me, so I send you." –John 20:21

Ministry is the active response to God's call. *Ministry* comes from the same root as *minus*, which means "less." Jesus said, "For who is greater: the one who is at the table or the one who serves? Is it not the one at the table? But I am among you as one who serves" (Luke 22:27). Paul, too, reminds us that our Lord "did not count equality with God as a thing to be grasped, but emptied himself, taking the form of a servant" (Phil. 2:6-7; RSV). Our call, then, will place us in the role of a minister, on God's behalf, in service to God's creation.

Christian ministry is more than simply doing good. Rather, it is something that Christ does in us and through us and that we do in and through Christ.[1]

As ministers of state act not on their own but on the authority of the states that send them, so, too, we act not on our own but on the authority of God who calls us. Jesus said, "You did not choose me, but I chose you. And I appointed you to go and bear fruit, fruit that will last . . ." (John 15:16).

We do not need to be ordained to have a ministry. *The Book of Common Prayer* specifies, "The ministers of the Church are lay persons, bishops, priests, and deacons."[2] All Christians are called to minister both to one another and to those around them by participating in God's work in the world. Ministry can occur between child and parent; among workers in an office or factory; between neighbors and friends. Hospitality may be ministry: welcoming the stranger, receiving and treating the people we encounter each day warmly and generously. Ministry includes prayer for one another. Ministry occurs in innumerable forms, some of which require ordination.

A minister is also one who waits, ready to respond as called. A waiter serves not only when running to the kitchen but also while waiting attentively. In this spirit, we await God's call to act in service to others.

Genuine ministry involves both giving and receiving. This reciprocity is central. Ministry "to" is patronizing, for it fails to acknowledge our own need; nor does it recognize the mutual nurturing experienced when we are brought to Christ through the people we serve.

Those who minister at a soup kitchen, for exampl often find themselves deeply enriched by those th serve.

Doing good things—volunteer work, for instance—may not be ministry if God is not the motivating force—even if the person doing them is a Christian.[3] On the other hand, if God is the motivating force, even those who do not consciously bear the name of Christ may participate in God's work. God used Cyrus, king of Persia, to release Israel from captivity, saying, ". . . I call you by your name, I surname you, though you do not know me" (Isa. 45:4). One task of the Christian, then, is to recognize, affirm, and celebrate God's call to others, including non-Christians. A true minister is "anybody who is the channel to others of God's love, and is willing to share something of the cost of that love; and whose eyes are open to perceive God's presence everywhere and in everybody."[4]

Whoever serves me must follow me, and where
I am, there will my servant be also. . . .
–John 12:26

Discernment

THREE

What Is Discernment?

Beloved, do not believe every spirit, but test the spirits to see whether they are from God. . . . –1 John 4:1

Discernment comes from the Latin word *discernere*, which means "to separate," "to distinguish," "to determine," "to sort out." In classical spirituality, discernment means identifying what spirit is at work in a situation: the Spirit of God or some other spirit. Discernment is "sifting through" our interior and exterior experiences to determine their origin.[1] Discernment helps a person understand the source of a call, to whom it is directed, its content, and what response is appropriate. Discernment also involves learning if one is dodging a call, is deaf to a call, or is rejecting a call.

Discernment is a gift from God.[2] But it also includes an intentional attempt on our part to hear God's call in our life.[3] It takes work; it is also a matter of grace. It involves our full humanity as well as communion with God.

Many voices call us: voices of culture, career, upbringing, worldview, peer pressure, ego, self-interest. These voices may be good in and of themselves yet may drown out the voice of God. How can we distinguish between God's call and other calls? How can we evaluate whether a call springs from a desire for security or comfort or success, rather than from God? How can we verify that a call comes from God?

No rules provide definitive answers to these questions.[4] And some rules that do exist provide poor or incomplete guidance. The experiences of the early Quakers illustrate this. One test some Quaker sects used to confirm God's call was that a "true" call was always contrary to one's own will.[5] The assumption that a "cross to the will"[6] meant taking up the cross of Christ often produced absurd results. For example, some Friends walked naked in the streets because it was "contrary to [their] own will or inclination" and, therefore, "in obedience to the Lord."[7] Another test was reliance on a selected passage of Scripture. Frequently, however, this meant (and can still mean) merely choosing some biblical passages and ignoring others to confirm a precharted course.[8]

The ability to discern comes from living the life of the Spirit, a process of growth involving an ever-greater integration of desires, feelings, reactions, and choices with a continuing commitment to abide in Christ. Indeed, through integrating the actions and relationships of life into one's identity with Christ we come to feel whether various impulses move us toward or away from the Spirit.[9] Discernment develops in a relationship with God, as one becomes rooted and grounded in the heart of God.[10] Thus, people who abide in the Lord are more likely to be able to hear and distinguish calls.[11]

As we grow in spiritual maturity, we move beyond the need for specific rules and answers into the darkness of God where we must act in faith rather than certainty. In discernment we move through and beyond our feelings, our thoughts, and our reasoning about what God wants of us, to be led by God's Spirit toward action. Discernment does not imply fully comprehending God's will,[12] but rather it raises the question, What is the next step God wants me to take?[13]

Discernment may be understood as "apprehending" rather than "comprehending."[14] Although discernment involves use of reason, the process is delicate and easily stifled by excessive analysis.[15] Pascal observes, "The heart has its reasons, that reason does not know."[16] Discernment of call involves intuition and insight, ". . . for that which has not been told them, they shall see, and that which they have not heard, they shall understand" (Isa. 52:15; RSV). As we respond in faith and action, we gain insight.

When we turn our hearts to God, we experience a reorientation of values deep within us. One of two things may happen. Either we become increasingly astute and wise as we live out our new orientation—we walk in the Spirit. Or, if we are not true to the new life that is rising within us—if we deny, repress, or live in contradiction to it—we invite internal havoc and trigger war within ourselves. Our lives may take on a frantic quality.[17]

Because the evidence and experiences on which we act are usually conflicting and ambivalent, and because we are by nature vulnerable to our capacity for self-deception, discernment is often tentative and uncertain.[18] We may not feel a great sense of having found the truth. Discernment can be like driving an automobile at night: the headlights cast only enough light for us to see the next small bit of road immediately in front of us.[19] Ultimately, discernment requires our willingness to act in faith on our sense of what God wants us to do.[20]

We need to risk making mistakes. We can dare to make mistakes because we know that God has forgiven us when we are wrong.[21] It is important that we act on what we have discerned, yet continue to listen in case we have heard incorrectly or incompletely. We need to be attentive and alert in order to hear and understand any call; then act, confident that God blesses even our mistakes.

. . . the word is very near you; it is in your mouth and in your heart, so that you can do it.
–Deut. 30:14 (RSV)

FOUR

What Conditions Help Discern God's Call?

. . . turn to the Lord your God with all your heart and with all your soul. –Deut. 30:10

God speaks, touches, and reveals in God's own way and in God's own time. Still, the presence of certain conditions, such as trust, prayer, and patience, makes discernment of God's call more likely.[1] Having or meeting these conditions does not mean that we *will* discern God's call, only that discernment becomes more likely.[2]

The conditions in this chapter apply not only to a person seeking discernment but to all who are trying to help that person. It is God's call, not mere decision-making, that we seek.[3] In order to discern which path is authentic, all involved need to desire to know God, to be willing to be pervaded by God's presence.

We need to go through a process that cleanses our vision to see what is true and frees our will to act on what we see.[4] Here are some ways we may prepare to hear God's call.

Trust

"Commit your way to the Lord; trust in him, and he will act." (Ps. 37:5)

First and foremost, we have to be willing to trust God and one another. Trust that God is present to us, speaks to us, is loving and merciful, and has work for us to do.[5] Trust that, in opening our hearts to others, we will encounter the Lord.[6] We need to act on the conviction that "all things work together for good for those who love God" (Rom. 8:28).

Listening

"O that my people would listen to me, that Israel would walk in my ways!" (Ps. 81:13)

Discernment involves listening. We must listen with open hearts and open minds,[7] especially to what we do not want to hear.[8] If discernment is to take place, we must let go of our preconceptions and expectations.[9] We must be willing to hear the appealing and the unappealing, the familiar and the unfamiliar. If we become selective, we may turn a deaf ear to God.

We need to listen with our bodies as well as with our minds, for God speaks to us through our pains and pleasures, through our wills, emotions, and senses.[10] To hear, we must listen with every fiber of our being.[11]

We must listen in silence, for stillness and silence enable us to hear. Elijah did not hear God in the mighty wind, or in the earthquake, or in the fire, but in a still, small voice (1 Kings 19:11-13).

Prayer

> "Seek the Lord and his strength; seek his presence continually." (Ps. 105:4)

Typically, we think of prayer as what we say to God, as in petition or in thanksgiving. Unlike the boy, Samuel, who said, "Speak, Lord, for your servant listens" (1 Sam. 3:10),[12] we often pray, "Listen, Lord, for your servant speaks." But prayer, especially prayer for discernment, involves listening. Through prayer we seek for ourselves total attentiveness to God's all-embracing presence. For God is found in the circumstances, the people, the things of daily life.[13] If we are aware of this, we will open our hearts, and, in this way, our whole life can become prayer in action.

Knowledge of Scripture

> "If you continue in my word . . . you will know the truth." (John 8:31-32)

Scripture is central to discerning call. The Bible records centuries of the developing historical and spiritual relationship between God and the people of God. The more familiar we are with Scripture, the more ready our access to the experience of God's people in history. Moreover, as the living Word of God, Scripture continues to communicate to us.

Humility

> "He leads the humble in what is right, and teaches the humble his way." (Ps. 25:9)

Humility comes from the same root as *humus*, meaning ground or earth. An attitude of humility is rooted in a true sense of one's self. Humility, grounded in self-knowledge, helps us avoid the distortions of inordinate self-confidence and exaggerated self-doubt.[14] A humble person is not someone who feels inferior but someone who is without pretense, who is down to earth. Humility lays the foundation for discernment because to be "humble in heart," as Jesus instructs us (Matt. 11:29), means that we will accept the uniqueness of our experience and the limited nature of our knowledge.[15] An attitude of humility allows us to accept dependence on God and one another and to be open to God's turning us in a new or unexpected direction.

Humility is not gained by seeking it directly nor obtained by focusing on one's faults and sins. Rather, it comes quietly to those who draw close to the Lord. As we experience God's greatness, we sense our own smallness. When we encounter God's wholeness, we realize our own incompleteness.[16]

Discipline and Perseverance

> "Those who seek me diligently find me."
> (Prov. 8:17)

It is essential for us to set aside a time and place to be in solitude so that we can be receptive to God's presence through Scripture, prayer, and silence.[17] This requires perseverance, especially for those who are not naturally inclined to solitude.[18]

Patience and Urgency

> "Be still before the Lord, and wait patiently. . . ."
> (Ps. 37:7)

Remember, it is God's call, not our call. So we need to be content to incline our ears with patience. In the meantime, let us offer up our prayers to God, asking God repeatedly to nurture our faith.

Still, while patience is called for at times, a sense of urgency is sometimes imperative. C.S. Lewis warns against progressing quietly and comfortably toward hell.[19]

"But everything has its time, and the main thing is that we keep step with God, and do not keep pressing on a few steps ahead—nor keep dawdling a step behind."[20]

Perspective

> "Is it lawful to heal on the sabbath?" (Matt. 12:10, RSV)

Do not make an idol of discernment. "The only priority worth having is knowing and loving God. Stay in the space of Love. Do not be lured out of it."[21] If discernment follows, fine; if not, so be it. Let it rest lightly. "Release your discernment from your ego and your expectations. Flow as a stream that is useful to those who can take" from it and is "in no way diminished by those who can't."[22]

At the same time, "Be true to what is inside. Put weight on it. Live by it. Hold it with sufficient tentativeness to be open to others . . . and with sufficient tenacity to live it out until moved differently."[23]

Impediments

Just as there are conditions favorable to discernment, there are impediments. Everything that gets in the way of hearing God's call is a barrier: "They served their idols, which became a snare to them" (Ps. 106:36). Obstacles arise from:

- *Culture.* Cultural values emphasizing competition, success, productivity, self-sufficiency, individualism, or material progress may impede discernment.

- *Prosperity.* Prosperity knits a person to the world.[24] "I spoke to you in your prosperity, but you said, 'I will not listen'" (Jer. 22:21).

- *Self-interest.* We need to free ourselves from the trap of self-interest that so grasps and clutches that it gets in the way of a free and open relationship with God and with others.[25] God begins where clinging to things ends.[26]

- *Self-absorption.* Ambition and self-absorption obstruct discernment.

- *Self-righteousness.* To be sure we are living in God's light is a sign of spiritual smugness and an impediment to discerning God's call.[27]

- *Desire for security.* Our desire for security and control interferes with our ability to hear God's call.

• *Desire for certainty*. To insist on an exact answer diminishes our freedom to listen.[28]

• *Human time frames*. Our own timetables impair our ability to let God point the way.

• *Self-doubt*. If we do not think we are good enough, we may not believe we can be useful to God and may be unable to pursue God's call. Moses was fortunate that God would not accept his response of personal inadequacy. We need to act on our best understanding of what God wants, praying that God will correct us if we have misunderstood.

And so, as we move from self-will to God's will, we place our lives in the hands of God. And then we find that God has work for us to do.

. . . you will find him if you search after him with all your heart and soul. –Deut. 4:29

FIVE

Is It God We Are Hearing?

Give your servant a heart to understand how to discern between good and evil. –1 Kings 3:9 (JB)

Access to what has been true for others can help us evaluate whether what we hear and see comes from God. The following insights are derived from varying traditions that span the centuries.

Where to Look

"Seeking God does not demand the unusual, the spectacular, the heroic."[1] It is in the here and now, the ordinary situation of normal life, that we find God. A true call is likely to be modest in scope. If we try to save the world, we become immobilized.[2]

Our Own Lives

There are stories from our lives through which God is telling us things we need to know. We need to identify those stories, tell them, and try to sort them out. We need "to read our own history, to see the turning points, the moments of change, the unfolding of God's plan for us at each new step of the way."[3]

By observing what we do, we can discover what we believe and value. Our past actions, our previous choices, the roads we have taken—all hold clues to who we are becoming. There is a connection between our temperaments and talents, and our call. We are called to work with the gifts we have been given. For this reason it is important to know our gifts. Paul warns, "Do not neglect the gift that is in you" (1 Tim. 4:14). Teilhard de Chardin suggests that when trying to draw out the full potential of a person, it is important to tap into those qualities that are unique.[4]

Still, discerning God's call is not the same as identifying one's gifts.[5] Unwilling to confront Pharaoh, Moses protested that he was not an eloquent speaker (Exod. 4:10). Yet God called Moses, saying, "Now go, I shall help you to speak and tell you what to say" (Exod. 4:12, JB). In discerning call, we need to be open to what Dag Hammarskjöld calls the "way of possibility,"[6] for we may not assess our gifts accurately, may not understand what is needed, may not see as God sees.[7]

The Desire for Change

Stability and change are factors to consider in discernment. Stability requires that we not run away from the place our battles are being fought.[8] If we cannot find God where we are, we may not be able to find God elsewhere.[9] Yet we need to be open to change. The call to change is ultimately nothing more and nothing less than a commitment to follow wherever God leads.[10]

There is an ebb and flow to life and work; at times our tasks are hard and difficult, at other times light and free. A long period of time during which our burdens are only heavy, when there is only ebb and no flow, may be a sign that we need to clarify our call. It may mean we are missing what God wants us to do amid the many things we are doing. If a call is a true call, we usually do not get burned out. A true call tends to be energizing.

It is important to know, however, that a person can be led by God into what John of the Cross calls a "dark night of the soul," a spiritual experience marked by great distress and prolonged tribulation.[11] Some of the signs of the Spirit seem to be absent. Yet other signs of the Spirit are present, though possibly difficult to see in the darkness. A person going through this kind of an experience needs to seek out someone with skill in this area. It is commonly assumed that a spiritual director is the best guide for a person experiencing spiritual darkness. Many spiritual directors, however, are not qualified to provide guidance in this area.[12] Anyone in a mysterious phase of spiritual darkness will need to seek help patiently, trusting that God will produce a proper guide at the appropriate time.

Assessing the Options

To consult moral rules such as those contained in the Ten Commandments can provide guidance, not to crush inner promptings and not to take their place, but to test them.[13] However, pride can make us cling to our understanding of a moral rule.[14] Thus, while moral rules provide capsules of wisdom tested by time, we must resist treating them as idols.[15]

It can be helpful to examine our ideas against opposing ideas. For example, if we feel a desire to do something, it can help to consider likely consequences were we to do the opposite.[16] Bear in mind that what could be a good decision for one person might be the wrong one for someone else.[17] What might be the right choice at one time could be the wrong one at another time.

God's purpose is unified. If it seems that God's messages are contradictory, we need to view the situation from a different or wider angle or step back to find a new vantage point. Still, it is good to be mindful that God's ways are not our ways (Isa. 55:8), and God may be calling us to act in a way we do not understand.[18]

The Needs of Others

In baptism we are incorporated into the Body of Christ, which makes us communal by definition. To quote Paul, "together [we] make a unity . . . building up the body of Christ" (Eph. 4:13, JB). Thus, the needs of the community are important to consider in evaluating a call.

Jesus frequently chose the humble, poor, rejected, and despised. They are often the preferred dwelling place of God—in them, we may meet God.[19] If we are hearing something that leads us to the disadvantaged, it may be a good indication that God is trying to get our attention.

> If you take away from the midst of you the yoke, the pointing of the finger . . . if you pour yourself out for the hungry and satisfy the desire of the afflicted, then shall your light rise in the darkness and your gloom be as the noonday. And the Lord will guide you continually. (Isa. 58:911, RSV)

Scripture

When we think that our Lord is speaking to us, it is prudent to determine if what we hear is consistent with Scripture.[20] If it is not, perhaps the voice we hear is not God's. Or, if it is God, we may be misunderstanding what is being said. Or we may be misinterpreting Scripture.

We need to bear in mind that every word spoken in the Bible is a partial and limited witness to truth.[21] We should not let our preferences silence any biblical voice, nor should we read the Bible merely to assure ourselves that we are right but, rather, to look for areas in which we have not been listening.[22] Take care to consider the context in which a book of Scripture was written. Accepting a passage of Scripture without considering its presuppositions can lead to distortion.[23]

While each generation must preserve the teaching that has been passed on, it must also add to this living tradition the wisdom derived from its own experience.[24] No one can hear the gospel except through the events of one's own time, for the Holy Spirit is a living teacher who does not merely repeat a tradition of the past.[25] Thus, it is good to beware of legalism and authoritarianism, always ready to see things in a new light.

Motives

A healthy skepticism of our own motives is a sign of spiritual maturity. For instance, many Christians have vied for the privilege of presiding at eucharist. Would they be so likely to vie to wash dirty feet?[26] We need to examine our motives for wanting to serve in a specific way. Christ's false friends are those who consider themselves his friends but who go about seeking Jesus for their own satisfaction.[27]

Signs of God's Call

God often speaks through signs. No single sign ensures that a particular understanding of God's will is correct. Neither is it likely that all signs will be present in any given situation. Nevertheless, signs can combine to provide an informed sense of where the Spirit is pointing. Some signs to watch for:

- Peace—the central sign. Peace does not mean an absence of trouble. Rather, it means a firm conviction, even in the midst of turmoil, that *the Lord is risen* and that "all shall be well."[28] Serenity is its manifestation. But beware of false peace. This can come from escaping an unhappy situation, denying painful realities, avoiding a cross, or making a decision (even one that is wrong) merely to terminate a crisis of indecision. If the peace endures through ups and downs, then we have confirmation that it is authentic.[29]

- Joy—a deep interior joy that is unselfconscious and uninhibited.[30]

- A temporary experience of disorientation, followed by calm and serenity.[31]

- Tears that are comforting and tranquilizing, rather than disturbing and fatiguing.[32]

- A sudden sense of clarity.

- Strands of experience that seemed unrelated begin to converge and fit together.

- Persistence—the message keeps recurring through different channels.

Through integrating our desires, feelings, reactions, and choices with our life in God, we may come to sense whether or not various impulses are from God. This clarity is known as "felt-knowledge."[33]

God's call may be heard through a spiritual experience. The experience may be unsought and unexpected but vivid and indelible.[34] It is so clear at the time it occurs that we would not think to question it.[35] At first it may leave us speechless, but later able to speak of it. It is attended by gratitude, love, and humility. A spiritual experience may include an image from God that lasts only an instant but is branded in us forever.[36]

Circumstance and coincidence may cause us to be in the right place at the right time to do God's work in a specific way. This may be a sign that God is calling us. So, too, if we seem to be the only ones aware of a concern and wonder why someone does not do something, it may be that we are being called to do it.

CAUTIONS

It is not possible to help everybody. Being endlessly available to anyone or everyone is good for no one.[37]

In times of inner turmoil, disturbance, sadness, or depression, be wary of making a change. Move slowly and carefully, for in such a time the way to a right decision can be obscured.[38]

Previous commitments demand serious consideration. Commitments generally, and especially commitments to children, spouse, and others, must be a factor in determining God's call and the timing and nature of one's response.[39] Watch out for feelings of peace that come from escape, even when accompanied by feelings of joy.[40]

Avoid being dominated by human timetables; it is God's time, not our time, that is our concern. If we are anxious or obsessed about the future, it may be a sign that we are out of touch with God's presence. In contrast, confidence in the future based on trust in God frees us to live fully in the present.[41]

The presence of fervor and passion for a particular path is not necessarily trustworthy—unless the zeal emanates from love of God. The real test is not how much we want to do something but how much love is a part of what we want to do.

A call may seem perfectly reasonable, but neither is this trustworthy. We must remember that we can deceive ourselves by reasoning.[42] Coming to a carefully reasoned conclusion does not mean we have discerned God's call.

We should beware of certainty, arrogance, and thoughts of superiority. Those who are positive about what is true may very well be deceived.[43]

If the apparent good that comes to us is accompanied by vanity, anxiety, irritability, resentment, condemnation, or condescension, it may be a sign that we are not hearing God's call.[44]

It is important to realize that the devil can operate in very subtle ways, appealing to our sense of what is good. One way to describe evil is as "segmented good." This suggests that we can be tempted to concentrate on one thing that is good while ignoring what is best for the whole.

You will know them by their fruits.
–Matt. 7:16

Community

SIX

Why Is Community Important in Discerning God's Call?

Where two or three are gathered in my name, there am I in the midst of them. –Matt. 18:20 (RSV)

Jesus lived his life in common with others, sharing and participating in God's work. He began his ministry by calling Simon, Andrew, and others to proclaim the Good News (Matt. 4:18-22; Mark 1:16-20). During his ministry he continued to gather men and women, and he ended his ministry by promising to be with them always (Matt. 28:16-20).

As followers of Jesus, we are called to live as Jesus did: in a community of faith. The word *community* comes from *communis*, meaning "common," and from *communicare*, meaning "to share or participate." Paul uses the metaphor of the Body of Christ to describe the interconnectedness of all members: "Now you are the body of Christ and individually members of it . . ." (1 Cor. 12:27). "If one member suffers, all suffer together with it; if one member is honored, all rejoice together with it" (1 Cor. 12:26). A life lived in common faith with others—in community—is central to Christianity.

God seeks a personal relationship with each of us and solitude is vital to our life in God. Jesus himself often went to a quiet place, alone, to pray (Mark 1:35; 6:46; 14:32-39). Yet Scripture makes a special point of bidding us to come together in God's name. Jesus said, "Where two or three are gathered in my name, there am I in the midst of them" (Matt. 18:20, RSV).

Something happens to us when we consult one another in Christian community.[1] In sharing our thoughts with others, surprising insights often emerge—opening our eyes to what we have not seen and our ears to what we have not heard.[2] This can transform and liberate us beyond our own narrow expectations. Both the one experiencing a call and those helping that person may express God's wisdom and grace in the process. "I will give you shepherds after my own heart, who will feed you with knowledge and understanding" (Jer. 3:15).

Although God calls each of us personally, as individuals we see only partially. Individual perception, reasoning, and understanding are always limited. Even a person who feels absolutely certain that a specific revelation comes from God may be mistaken as to how it is to be applied.[3] Because God often reveals part of the picture to one person and another part to another person, it is prudent to consult one another to discern God's counsel, guidance, and direction, even if there is no apparent reason to do so.[4] While circumstances sometimes require us to act without consulting others, the danger of arrogance and error in proceeding on our own can be great.[5]

Another role for community is all but essential in order for us to recognize and respond to our call. It is to encourage us in our love of God and to keep us from becoming conformed to the world. How are we to resist the powerful attraction of the world's values: love of money, power, social approval, security, comfort, success? For many of us, the answer is only by meeting together regularly in the name of the Lord, probably in small groups, and thereby experiencing God's presence and love. In this company, in the light and presence of Christ, we can see through the sham of worldly values yet share in God's love for all creation. In this company, we are strengthened to live as God's people. Here, we can perceive truth and be obedient and faithful to our call in spite of the pull of the world.

Just hours before his death, Jesus prayed for his disciples:

> Holy Father, protect them in your name that you have given me, so that they may be one, as we are one. . . . I have given them your word, and

> the world has hated them because they do not belong to the world, just as I do not belong to the world. I am not asking you to take them out of the world, but I ask you to protect them from the evil one. They do not belong to the world, just as I do not belong to the world. Sanctify them in the truth; your word is truth. As you have sent me into the world, so I have sent them into the world. And for their sakes I sanctify myself, so that they also may be sanctified in truth. (John 17:11, 14–19)

By meeting together in the Lord's name, we claim that prayer for ourselves. And we can accept truth and God's call for us without being overwhelmed by the judgment and values of the world.

Nevertheless, we should bear in mind that from the very start our Christian communities have had their weaknesses as well as strengths, their errors as well as insights. Thus, advice, judgment, and support from a community must be received critically, as well as with love and respect. This can be particularly evident when a person in the community feels called to a prophetic role.

The prophet is not an easy person for the community to accept. It can be a trial for a community to hear the prophet's voice and acknowledge that it comes from God, since the very task of the prophet is to challenge the status quo. A hundred years before the

Civil War, John Woolman felt called to be an abolitionist among the Quakers, but he also felt that he should not undertake this without the blessing of his Meeting.[6] As a result, Woolman wrestled with his faith community over this issue for two years; many members of the community owned slaves. While many did not agree with the abolitionist position, they came to believe that Woolman did have a call and promised to support him and his family while he responded to it. During the two years Woolman stayed and presented his call, the community's members were deeply affected. Because of Woolman's faithfulness to his call and willingness to work out that call in the community, the Quakers eventually came to oppose slavery.[7]

We can never achieve wholeness simply by ourselves but only together with others.[8] Consequently, as we involve the community in discerning call, God enlivens and strengthens both us and the community.

. . . the saints together make a unity in the work of service, building up the body of Christ.
–Eph. 4:13 (JB)

SEVEN

Discerning Call in Community

Let us consider how to stir up one another to love and good works, not neglecting to meet together . . . but encouraging one another. –Heb. 10:24-25 (RSV)

As our life in God deepens, and our knowledge of call and discernment broadens, we may find ourselves helping each other wrestle with issues of call when gathered informally. Likewise, groups meeting for specific purposes such as Bible study may at times focus on a question of call for one of the members. The more a Christian community becomes grounded in prayer and discernment, the more this kind of discussion will take place spontaneously.

Even so, some people will find it easier to get the kind of help they need if the community offers a specific structure, as described in appendix 1.

Whether a group is formal or informal, spontaneous or structured, it can help to consider how to proceed.

First, people seeking help need to provide some information about their own faith journeys. God communicates with each of us in a way that is unique. The more fully we can delineate patterns of God's communication over the span of our lives, the more effectively we can evaluate what is transpiring at the moment.

Once the person asking guidance has laid out the issues and sketched in the appropriate background, those present need to identify their own biases relative to the situation. We all have histories that shape our outlooks. What we have to say needs to be understood against the background of those histories. Ideally, each person present will silently reflect on questions such as these: What colors my perception of this person or issue? Would it be constructive for me to articulate my bias? We are more receptive to God's Spirit in an atmosphere that is honest and open, relaxed and gentle.

An additional consideration: we normally relate to some people in a group more readily than to others. Psychologically, we tend to turn off the people we most need to hear.[1] The people to whom we are least attracted often have the most to teach us. If we identify those to whom we are least drawn, we can make a special effort to listen to them attentively.

Prayerful listening may be the most important aspect of discernment. Paul Tillich wrote, "No human relation, especially no intimate one, is possible without mutual listening."[2] In the same way, no relationship with God, especially not an intimate one, is possible without mutual listening. As we listen to God in prayer and through one another, we grow in Christian community and in our sense of God's path for us.[3]

The silence of prayerful listening is not so much the absence of talk as it is presence to the Word. "We keep silence solely for the sake of the Word . . . to honor and receive it."[4] Frequent times of silence are important during a discernment gathering:

> There is a wonderful power of clarification, purification, and concentration upon the essential thing in being quiet. . . . This is true as a purely secular fact. But silence before the Word leads to right hearing, and thus also to right speaking of the Word of God at the right time.[5]

Members of the group help the person seeking discernment by listening prayerfully and raising questions concerning the issue. Prayerfully formulated questions invite the movement of God's Spirit. While there may be no clear answers, the right question can be crucial. Answers can shut down growth; good questions encourage growth. Answers sometimes terminate our listening; questions stimulate further listening.

A goal of a discernment group is to reach spiritual consensus, which the Quakers call "sense of the meeting." For the Quakers, this consensus is a way of sensing the will of God.[6] Spiritual consensus incorporates rational consideration, but comes most especially through prayerful listening.[7]

Consensus is not the same as unanimity, and it is not group decision making. Not everyone must actually agree, but no one can be so opposed as to feel obligated to resist. Since anyone can block consensus, the process gives each person power and requires each person to exercise that power responsibly.

When people feel a strong commitment to stand their ground, that desire compels them to reexamine their position and present it more clearly. Consensus relies on waiting prayerfully until everyone can find a position that all can embrace. No votes are taken. No one wins or loses.

In pursuing consensus, we have to try to build bridges and look for new ways to approach situations. We need to listen carefully to pinpoint areas of agreement and build on them. We need to look for ways to reconcile differing points of view, perhaps accommodating opposing sides of an issue. Efforts to arrive at consensus often produce unexpected results.

People meeting with a discernment group may come to feel that what they are hearing does not come from God. This, too, is discernment. For example, a person may unconsciously identify a course of action as coming from God in order to escape an intolerable situation. That person may come to understand that getting out of the situation is necessary but is not a call. Or a person may realize that certain decisions do not involve a call and simply need to be made. Or a consensus may emerge that a discernment group has gone far enough, leaving the issue of call to future resolution in God's own time. Understanding that a call does not come from God, or even seeing that an issue is not as clear as it once seemed, can quiet the cacophony within, creating stillness and space, fostering silent, listening hearts where, finally, they come to hear the Lord speak.

And so, as we help one another wrestle with issues of call, our knowledge of call and discernment broadens, and our life in God deepens.

Now the whole group of those who believed were of one heart and soul. . . . –Acts 4:32

EIGHT

Support for Ministries

Moses' father-in-law said to him, "What you are doing is not good. You will surely wear yourself out, both you and these people with you. For the task is too heavy for you; you cannot do it alone." –Exod. 18:17-18

A wise swimmer does not cross a difficult channel without a boat close behind, with those aboard watching for signs of danger or weariness and providing words of encouragement along the way. Nor does a prudent climber scale a mountain alone, without companions to hold the rope and help along the way. Neither should one minister alone.

Ministry—lay or ordained—requires support. Without support, we may become lonely, bored, or weary. We may feel trapped by the tasks we have undertaken or find ourselves unable or unwilling to ask for help. Without support, ministry may become lost. Without support, we may become lost.

Whether support comes from a single person—a friend, companion, colleague, mentor, or adviser—or from a group, the key element is thoughtful attention. In order to respond to God's call effectively, we need time and occasions to talk about concerns and issues of vocation, to refine the call further, to be challenged, to be encouraged in a knowing and sustaining way, to be recognized, to be affirmed. Without time for talking, praying, and sharing, support can dwindle into superficial well-wishing or irrelevance or fade away altogether. Thus, the quality of the support we receive can make a vast difference as we face inevitable doubts, discouragements, and disappointments.

There are at least four ways to support and be supported in ministry: spiritually, psychologically, physically, and financially. The spiritual includes prayer, study of Scripture, and opportunities for reflection. The psychological involves affirming and understanding the person behind the ministry. The physical encompasses such diverse possibilities as offering a hug for encouragement or babysitting so that parents can pursue a particular ministry. The financial means putting our earthly treasure where our heart is—which is to say, funding ministry where funding is needed.

A person may find support in an existing group, such as one for Bible study, book discussion, or prayer. For example, if a sense of call arises from participation in a Bible study group, the relationships of trust and the shared commitments to Christian living within that group could provide a strong foundation for support.

Indeed, a person in such a group may elicit the aid of the group when first embarking on discernment leading to ministry. Another person's sense of call might emerge from a group initiated to work through some crucial issue—illness, marriage or divorce, loss of or search for a job. That group's understanding of the person's struggle, motivations, and discoveries could provide a foundation for effective support of ministry.

In contrast, another person may be exercising a vocation with no group to support it. For this person, a separate group of people with similar ministries may be helpful. Support based on participation or experience in the same ministry can be effective, as colleagues can supply insights, empathy, and experiential knowledge that others, however well intentioned, cannot offer. A group of this kind might spring up naturally among people engaged in the same ministry: an emergency food or tutoring program, for example. The pattern is not identical for everyone, and the support group, whatever its origin, needs to listen closely to the different tones and overtones of call that may sound at different stages in a person's life.

A support group need not focus on a single person. For example, a group may find mutual support working on a single issue or complex of similar issues. Or a group may find ministry in their occupations and choose to meet to maintain a strong connection between their work and their faith. A mutual support group such as this has the added benefit of offering all members of the group the opportunity to provide as well as receive support.

Some may find their principal support coming from people or groups that have no connection with the church, in which case they will need to discover other ways to connect their ministry with the community of faith.

Support for ministry may take many forms, occur on different levels, come from various sources. But there must be support. If there is no existing form of support for a ministry or none readily available, a person called to that ministry needs to consult with the community to find support—ideally even before embarking on the ministry.[1]

Finally, in supporting ministry we need to be clear about just what is being supported—the person or the ministry. Personal issues and events have an inevitable impact on ministry, and pastoral concern and attention are inseparable from support. However, the intention here is to discover how to support a person in ministry, how to keep that ministry faithful to one's own call.

We need to nurture Christ in each person— individually, in small groups, and as responsible members of the larger Body of Christ. Ideally, support for ministry will begin where our life together begins—when we gather for worship. Regular worship together is the heartbeat of ministry, giving life and strength to our day-to-day efforts to respond to God's call. Said another way, the various groups supporting ministry in a Christian community are as spokes on a wheel; coming together for corporate worship brings us to the hub.

The whole body is fitted and joined together, every joint adding its own strength. –Eph. 4:16 (JB)

NINE

Accountability for Ministries

Brothers and sisters, be all the more eager to confirm your call and election. –2 Pet. 1:10

In the parable of the talents, Jesus tells us that we are accountable for what we do with our gifts and our time. To be accountable means to answer to someone who cares about what we do and how we do it—someone who has an investment in our work. To be accountable for ministry means answering to those who invest in our ministry. Wise ministers—lay or ordained—encourage accountability, for without it, they have no community of support. Thus, the minister and support group must be responsible to one another, to the community that sustains them, and, ultimately, to God.

The ministry support group does not exist to provide the minister with a warm, pleasant group of friends.

Rather, the group comes together to help a person follow a particular way of living out their faith or their values. Like support, accountability has several dimensions, of which the spiritual is the most important and the most easily overlooked. We are accountable not only for doing our ministry but also for the spirit in which we do it. If our ministry becomes disconnected from our prayer life, if we cease to see God in the people to whom or with whom we minister, if we no longer do the work of our ministry with joy and love and to God's glory, we may have lost touch with our call.

Changes in the spirit with which we do our ministry are subtle; they may be difficult for us to notice and for those around us to notice—and, once noticed, perhaps even more difficult to talk about. For this reason, it is not easy to provide accountability without a close and continuing support group or relationship within the community of faith. Thus, in discernment, in support, in ministry, we need to work together to help one another in our common journey. We are companions on the way, not adversaries. Faithfulness to our callings demands that we be honest and responsible with each other, to keep from veering aside into dead ends and to remind one another in whose name we travel.

As weighty as the idea of accountability can be, we need not be intimidated by it. Accountability builds relationships of healthy interdependence. Support and accountability are closely intertwined, each being an integral part of the other. If we are not accountable to others for our ministry, especially for its spiritual dimension, how can they support us? If we cannot rely on their support, how can we find the courage to be accountable?

A word of caution is in order. The positive sense of call that the minister feels can lead to the dangerous attitude that the minister is accountable to God alone and need not pay attention to the reservations and concerns of those providing support. Conversely, the positive sense of "ownership" that the support group develops for the minister and vocation can turn into the dangerous notion that the minister is accountable only to that support group. Be wary of either attitude.

A healthy Christian community will encourage its members to become aware of one another and accountable to one another. We need to do everything possible to fill the community with an attitude of concern for one another. The genuine call of any person in a Christian community is rightly the concern of all—and a shared responsibility.

> *. . . they called the church together and related all that God had done with them. . . .* –Acts 14:27

Stories of Call

TEN

God Calls Each of Us

The authors invited each of the five writers whose stories follow to speak of their own experiences of God's call—what led the writer to move in a new direction, and what happened as a result.

In *Always Listening*, a woman reflects on her lifelong call to seek and hear God's voice and the confirmations of joy and peace that followed her decisions. The writer in *God's Call to Love* is slowly drawn to return to God and later has an experience through which she understands that, in her own life, she is called to extend God's love to others.

Discovering the Path Forward tells of the unfolding of a life's journey as far back as choosing a college major—viewed in retrospect through the signs of a call—and the realization that those signs had not always been visible. In *The Journey Begins Again*, a writer experiences God's call in multiple forms over decades and learns as a result to incorporate Buddhist, Christian, and atheist phases of his spiritual journey into his life and practice.

In the final story, *A Call to Contemplative Prayer*, a young woman finds a tract in a church that calls her to a specific breathing prayer. In the ninth decade of life, she arrives at a new form of contemplative practice based upon a "wordless word."

I—Always Listening

I love the phrase "the *practice* of spiritual discernment." It suggests an act, an ongoing activity, a deliberate effort to try to hear God's call in your life. For me, seeking God, hearing God's voice, and finding God's direction and path is a state of being. In a real and powerful way, it is my purpose, and my call.

As the only girl in a family of six, I was closest to my mother. She taught me, through her love but also through her words, that God is here with us. While dying, she said to me, "God has been right there beside me my whole life, and that is a great gift." This gift—the knowledge of God's presence—she gave to me. She taught me to know that God is here and will guide me if I will only listen.

I also know, although I cannot say that I was taught this—that we are put on this earth to work, to *do* something. And so, regularly, I am on the journey of questioning: am I doing what I should be doing? Am I spending my time, my days, my energy on what I am called to do?

Raised Catholic, I attended Mass every weekend (a practice that admittedly has diminished over my adult life), yet Sunday Mass was not when I found myself praying. To the contrary, "church" was an event, an experience—and often an opportunity to feel the pain of the world, the struggle of living.

The praying was in the conversations with God, in listening to hear God's voice. Alone—waking, exercising, working, cooking, awaiting the coming of sleep, contemplating life, the decisions of the day, the dreams for tomorrow. Looking back, I feel deeply the power of these conversations. I felt—and feel—connected. Many of my life decisions have been accompanied by feelings of peace, joy, and at times, even tears—for me, signs of God's presence in my life.

I appreciate that one could interpret my words as presumptuous. How is it that I can feel this close to God? How can I know that God calls me? I do not apologize. I only know that it is true. My call is to seek God, to hear and respond to God's voice, over the course of lifetime. It is the journey that I am on, wherever it takes me.

II—God's Call to Love

I grew up in a large family on a farm in a small town in New England. There were always kids around, and we had the freedom to roam through meadows, wade in brooks, climb trees, build forts in the hay bales, and ride bikes for miles. There were certainly rules and structure, of course. Looking back, though, mostly there was independence. Later, I attended boarding school and welcomed the new type of independence that came with it—independence of thought and independence to choose a direction for my life from a broader range of opportunities that emerged from the profound changes in society in the 1960s and '70s.

Like many in my generation, I regularly attended a mainstream Protestant church with my family and believed what I was taught as a child. Then, in my late teens, I stopped attending church. While I did not have any particular beef with God or the church, I was free to skip the service and so I did. Gradually that hardened into a deliberate choice as I realized that much of my childhood faith made no sense, as my parents were drawn into fundamentalism and put pressure on me to take up their beliefs. Without any firm conviction and with many demands of a busy life, it was certainly easier not to engage—with any of it.

Following college and a couple of years working, I went to law school. I got married, practiced law, bought a house, and raised a family. To all appearances my life was successful—a career, a marriage, children, friends. It all seemed good. And yet, in moments of quiet reflection, I knew something was missing. I would occasionally feel twinges of God's pull in my life. I would remember moments when I had felt I had been in the presence of the Divine breaking into the chapel at school at dusk just to sit quietly, singing magnificent anthems in the school choirs, in the decision to major in religion in college. I remembered a book I received when I was three that in words and pictures spoke of God's loving presence in every living creature and throughout the universe. These were memories that did not include rules or judgment. I longed for the understanding of those moments as the simple grace of God's unconditional love, and I longed for words to describe them in ways my family could hear.

I made no response to those moments over a period of thirty years. Then cracks started to appear in the marriage. In the long lead up to an inevitable breakup, I remember thinking (was it praying?), "God, if anything happens to this marriage, I will go back to church." It did, and I did. "Go back to church" I now understand was a promise to respond to those unbidden moments of reflection and memory, to engage them, and to enter into a relationship with God. Their persistence over the years was a sign of God's Spirit seeking to awaken me to God's love. The peace I felt when at last I stopped resisting the call to God's love was a sure and certain sign of the Spirit.

Looking back, I was also able to recognize the presence of the Spirit guiding me through love. Years before, during a dark time in my life, one of my children had serious behavioral issues. My child's health care provider directed me to have a frank talk with the child about consequence and impacts of behavior. I had no idea what I would say or how. I could have spoken to my child in a harsh and punishing way and justified it as "tough love." Instead, my response, though stern, was loving and nonjudgmental—and heard by my child. In the aftermath of that conversation, we made many changes. While we had no assurances at the time that they would be successful, all of us knew that the choices were all made in love.

Only years later did I make the connection that God *is* love and was calling to me to love through and throughout this experience. This led me to a new understanding of God as a loving and compassionate God who loves all God's people, declares all of God's creation good and yearns for us to realize heaven on earth—in this life. This was so different from the faith of my childhood, and I struggled to accept that God's love for every person includes me. Sometimes I still do.

So it was a wonderful, exhilarating moment on New Year's morning over a decade ago, in the transition from sleep to wakefulness, that I heard a voice softly but clearly saying, "I love you." It is still thrilling writing it now. After several days had passed, I shared this experience with my best friend, who immediately replied, "And God loves through you." *God loves through me*. In that *aha!* moment, I comprehended fully that God's love for me is both inward focused and outward focused. Jesus's final commandment to "love one another as I have loved you" took on fuller meaning in that moment.

This was the completion of God's call to love. It began with the prompting to return to a relationship with God and the realization that the Spirit of God's love had been with me; continued with the experience of the blessed assurance of God's love for me; and finally led to the specific call that, through me, God's love is to be extended to all others. It has made a huge difference as I strive to let love guide my life.

III—Discovering the Path Forward

I was born in a Midwest city in the Rust Belt, the son of a steelworker and a stay-at-home mom who occasionally worked part-time jobs. Though I loved the outdoors, played basketball, and ran track, books were my first love. I started out reading comic books as a child and anything else I could get my hands on, including a children's encyclopedia and the backs of cereal boxes at the kitchen table.

As a teenager, I began to have a sense that my life had to have meaning, that there was something specific for me to do. In high school, I decided to become a lawyer for the purpose of helping others. After my freshman year in college, I declared a major in political science, the natural stepping-stone to law school. Then one day, in the fall of my sophomore year, while working at the campus library, I found myself talking to a student about a college major that involved reading the "Great Books" in religion, philosophy, and science, in small classes with discussions and oral exams. As it happened, I found myself in conversation over the next several days with other students about the same program. These students did not know one another; the conversations were coincidental. While I still loved to read, I had no idea what these important-sounding books were. Yet I distinctly remember being drawn to switch my major to this program. I did, not really knowing how I came to the decision, only that it felt like the right one.

Years later, I learned about signs that indicate a call is coming from God. Persistence is one: when a message keeps recurring through different channels. Felt-knowledge, from the Spanish word *sentir*, is another. This is that knowledge that you feel deep inside, as in the heart having its reasons "which reason does not know," in the words of Blaise Pascal, whose work I studied. In deciding to switch to a Great Books major, I heard a persistent message from different students about the program and experienced a "felt-knowledge" that it was the right way to go. I did not name what I felt as a call from God; I just sensed that it was the path ahead and took it. It was only later, in looking back, that I realized the significance of the decision, and the path that it set before me.

The books that I ended up reading for the next three years invited me to think about life, God, relationships, and meaning on my own terms, to seek to understand who I am, and what I am to do. They helped me to relate to myself, to others, to God, and to the life ahead. One professor in particular taught that life is less a process of decision-making and more one of discovery. This idea took root deeply within me. Ever since, I have been seeking to discover the path forward, always with the idea that there is something or something more I am called to do.

Here is one example. Decades after graduation, I became a member of a church that was part of a nonprofit group running a homeless shelter. One day, my pastor asked me if I would like to serve on the board of directors for the shelter. I remember the day like it was yesterday. I had long wanted to do something for those who were homeless, moved by the words of Matthew 25, that we should care for "the least of these among us." I said "yes" immediately, almost before the question was asked. I felt a sudden sense of clarity that this was what I was called to do.

Clarity, I had learned, is another sign of God's call, especially if grounded in scripture.

Two years after joining the board, I became its president and undertook a study on the needs of the homeless in the community for emergency and transitional housing. Four years later, I became the organization's project director for planning, design, and construction of a new homelessness prevention center. The project involved engaging and educating city, county, and state officials on our responsibilities to those without housing and the need for funding the project. This was in addition to my day job as an attorney. In all, I spent a decade as a volunteer for the board and project, yet none of it felt like work. As I have also learned, a true call is energizing.

To be sure, this is not to say that that I have always discovered the right paths. I married because it seemed like the next logical step in the relationship, not realizing that reasonableness is an undependable guide. The marriage did not last. I have made other ill-advised decisions in times of depression, hoping that change would light the darkness, not realizing that in such times, one should be especially cautious of making a change. I learned the hard way that God speaks to us through all of our senses and also our feelings.

Discovering the path forward is a lifelong adventure of walking in uncertainty, looking for signs, trusting that God will lead me rightly, even if, as in the Merton prayer, "I may know nothing about it."

IV—The Journey Begins Again

I grew up in rural central New York State, in a middle-class family that had just enough extra money to eat out once per month. My mom was ahead of her time—"spiritual but not religious" before that was a thing. My dad was an agnostic from an Irish Catholic family. Out of love for my mom's father, a faithful Episcopalian and community activist, my parents raised me in the Episcopal Church until I was about ten years old. After that, we were essentially unchurched, except maybe on Easter. My personal fascination with faith led to friendships with evangelical Christians in middle school and college, and a college minor in religion while earning a degree in computer science. (I was a geek from a young age.) For the past twenty years, I've developed news applications and websites for a major news media company based in northern Virginia, near Washington, DC.

My initial experience of what I would interpret as a "call" from God was shortly after I was diagnosed with clinical depression. The assessment itself was a relief because it made clear that *something* was wrong. The psychiatrist who diagnosed me was also a therapist. In one of our sessions, as we discussed my own habits that contributed to my unhappiness, he observed that I seemed to have a notable lack of mindfulness.

My immediate reaction to this observation was: *yes, that sounds right*. I felt a strong sense that I had been seen and understood clearly and that this was an opportunity for me to grow. As a former student of world religions, I knew that nobody knew more about mindfulness than the Buddhists. I was fortunate to find a thriving Tibetan *sangha* that became my first spiritual home. Thus began three years as a committed practicing Buddhist, a core thread in my spiritual tapestry that remains central to this day. Ironically, it took me many years, and multiple twists and turns in my spiritual journey before I began truly to invest in daily mindfulness practice and reap the benefits in my life and relationships.

A second time I sensed God's call was a year after moving to the DC area, failing to find a home *sangha*, and realizing that I was no longer a practicing Buddhist. My wife and I were visiting her grandparents and I learned that the plan was to spend all of Christmas Day at their Southern Baptist church. To be honest, I was not looking forward to it, but I was amazed: in an economically depressed little town, the church threw open its doors to all comers and served a properly abundant Baptist potluck—without cost. This had such an impact on me that I felt a strong sense of call: *maybe I should give the Church a second try*. When I got home, I reconnected with the tradition of my early childhood by seeking and finding an

Episcopal church in my town. Within a few months, I was taking a newcomers' class on my way to reaffirming my confirmation. When I heard the words "all baptized Christians are called to ministry," my life changed forever. I realized that I needed to search for the meaning of my personal call to ministry.

Another experience of God's call occurred two years later when, at the suggestion of my pastor, I began reading books on the topic of "emerging" and "missional" church. I remember feeling an *irresistible pull* toward these innovative and experimental ways of "doing church." To my surprise, I found a nearby "emerging" church that became the focus of my life for the next fifteen years. Among the people of this church, whom I came to love as my sisters and brothers, I learned more than I could have imagined about the creative ways that God is always at work in the world, among God's people, blessing and changing lives. From our experimental worship, which drew in folks who had been pushed away by traditional churches, to our "barn raisings" where the whole congregation engaged in "service worship" while working together on projects to help people in our community, my sense of the kingdom of God was made brand new.

Five years later, I found myself once again plunged into the depths of clinical depression. This time, paradoxically, I believe that *God was calling me to let go of God.* (Or to let go of my ideas and expectations about God.) I spent nine months of depression staring into the abyss of my own mortality and emerged from that darkness ready and able to let go of my need to live forever—and also (I thought) of my need for God. I became a fervent atheist. Looking back on this period, I believe it was a vital stage of my spiritual journey—the only way I could let go of some attachments that I truly needed to relinquish.

These days, I honor and incorporate the Buddhist, Christian, and atheist phases of my spiritual journey into my life, my practice, and my path. I worship with my Episcopal Church, practice Buddhist-style mindfulness meditation daily, and bring an atheist's skeptical approach to my continuing journey. I look back on my encounters with God's call, and I note that in many of them, I began in a period of emotional, psychic, and spiritual turmoil, and only gradually found my way to a place of equanimity, peace, and joy. Each time, years after arriving there, the journey began again.

V—A Call to Contemplative Prayer

I grew up in New York State, with parents who were baptized Christians but rarely went to church for the first ten years of my life. My father was often transferred from one town to another, so sometimes we never connected with any church at all. Nevertheless, my mother taught me at a very young age to kneel by my bed at night to say the "Now I Lay Me Down to Sleep" prayer and then ask God to bless my family members by name.

When I was in first and second grade, we lived in Corning. My father would drop me off for Sunday school each week, then return to take me home. I must have had innate spiritual yearnings because once I was tucked into bed for the night with no one else around, I remember conducting rituals to express my passionate love for God.

Fast-forward to the middle of winter when I was in fourth grade. We moved to the village of Monticello in the Catskill Mountains. Right away, my father became an active member of St. John's Episcopal Church. By the beginning of the next academic year, he was superintendent of the Sunday school, which marks the moment I began to put down roots in the church.

In sixth grade, I was confirmed. The next Sunday I started to go to the eight o'clock communion service on my own. Receiving communion was a serious matter to me. It included the obligation to forgive anyone I felt had wronged me. The following year my mother began going to church with me.

My devotion to God continued until my sophomore year of college when my moral compass went haywire and my affection for the church turned hostile.

Happily, by the end of my senior year, my rebellion subsided. I was ready to return to church.

After graduating from college, I headed to Boston, found a place to live, got a job, and started to attend nearby Trinity Church, Copley Square. Soon I decided to make it my parish home. I wrote a note to my rector requesting a letter of transfer—a request that typically is fulfilled as a matter of form. Strangely, he replied that he would not transfer me to Trinity, that I had to go to the Church of the Advent in Beacon Hill. I complied.

Inside the door of the Advent was a tract rack where I happened upon a pamphlet that introduced me to a breathing prayer. It consisted of four short phrases that incorporated the following practice: inhale, silently praying phrase one; exhale saying phrase two; inhale phrase three; exhale phrase four. In the days and weeks that followed, I prayed this prayer over and over. At the time, I had no idea what contemplative prayer was, yet this pamphlet initiated a call to it.

I began repeating the prayer on and off both day and night. Soon the prayer was taking root in me. After two or so years, it had taken on a life of its own. Time and time again, for the next sixty years, when I found myself in a difficult situation or had serious concern for another person's predicament, the prayer would automatically spring to life, becoming a channel of insight that showed a way forward, bringing with it a soothing sense of calm.

Then one day, about a year ago and without warning, the well went dry: the prayer no longer worked. The efficacy of other verbal aids such as mantras and the sacred word I used in centering prayer also vanished. A mild feeling of despair slowly fell over me and lingered, when, all at once it struck me that *words* had become an impediment to my life in the Spirit. I needed a "wordless word."

As it happens, recently I had stumbled upon the concepts that our unconscious is embedded in our body, and that our "spiritual heart" holds thoughts and emotions that are fully physical. These ideas gave rise to a sense that this "wordless word" needed to be physical rather than verbal. It had to emanate from my entire body rather than from my head. Initially, it took a sustained, strenuous, and wrenching effort to awaken the cells of my body to the spiritual energy that is all-encompassing. Now, as I write these words, more than a year has passed. Now it requires only a gentle interior physical nudge to pull me back to God's all-encompassing presence. Day or night—whether standing, sitting, walking, or lying down—at random times, I summon forth my wordless word.

This new way of practicing contemplative prayer is by no means on automatic pilot. Too often, I tend to drift away. I need to keep reminding myself to stay physically tuned in. Even so, the wordless word is profoundly affecting my life in God. It is infusing me with a visceral sense of communion with other people. Beyond that, what astonishes me most is that insights often surface to guide me before I ever knowingly ask.

This transition over the past year overlapped and merged with my awakening to cosmic spirituality. With the Christian narrative deeply embedded in me, my sense of Christ is busting through the boundaries. No longer is my life in the Spirit bound by walls that separate faith traditions nor by the walls that separate genders, races, cultures, and epochs. As I write these words at the age of eighty-five, my life in God keeps changing. It keeps expanding. I sense myself as part of the universe, connected through time and space to all that is, all that ever was and all that ever will be. Filled with a mysterious energy, I find myself moving full speed ahead into the future.

Epilogue: Hearts to Listen

"Live the questions," urges Rainer Maria Rilke. "Perhaps then, someday far in the future, you will gradually, without even noticing it, live your way into the answer."[1]

How can we hear God's call? What could hearing it mean as we live day to day? How can we help each other hear God's voice and follow where it leads? In the end, the questions posed by this book cannot be answered by any book. Rather, answers emerge within our hearts as we live the questions. Understanding that God calls us, preparing our hearts and minds to discern God's call, and meeting with others for insight and support helps us to live these questions.

Still, as our understanding of discernment deepens, we may discover the need to find or to create a specific structure to help us hear our own call, or to help others hear theirs. The appendices offer practical suggestions for this purpose. Appendix 1 provides time-tested guidelines for working with a Listening Hearts discernment group. Any organization or group that finds the underlying principles of this book in harmony with its own—including a church, diocese, retreat center, or informal collection of spiritual seekers—can make a discernment group available to individuals wrestling with real-life issues such as family problems, moral or ethical dilemmas, work-related difficulties, job changes, or the general direction of their lives.

Appendix 2 presents types of questions for an individual seeking or struggling to hear a call to consider. While the questions have been developed to use in the context of a discernment group, they also serve as a source for individual exploration of call.

Appendix 3 describes the research method used in writing the nine chapters of the original edition, which remain essentially as they appeared thirty years ago. The manner in which the authors went about their work set the tone for the entire book. Concluding appendix 4 explains the value of cultivating a culture of spiritual discernment and offers suggestions for doing so.

May these appendices serve as a guide to living a life of discernment in community.

Appendices of Practical Suggestions

Appendix 1
Guidelines for a Discernment Group

A discernment group works best if those serving as discerners are trained in prayerful listening, familiar with varied approaches to meditation, understand the concept of spiritual consensus, and are alert to signs of God's call. For information on programs and resources that prepare leaders to train discerners, go to www.listeninghearts.org.

What Is a Discernment Group?

A discernment group consists of the *focus person* (the person who has requested discernment in relation to an issue they are wrestling with) and three trained *discerners*. One of the discerners is designated as the *convener*.

The group gathers, not for discussion or dialogue, but for prayer. The prayer is in silence, in listening, in waiting for the Lord to speak through them. The intent is not decision-making, but to walk with God while living the question. The discerners avoid counseling techniques, advice, or commentary. They limit themselves to **simple, prayerfully conceived questions** posed only after quiet reflection. The guidelines that follow can help persons who assimilate them and abide by them to work effectively as discerners.

A discernment group meeting is **absolutely confidential** unless the focus person expressly chooses otherwise. If the focus person wants to initiate talk with a member of the group at a future date, that is permissible. No discerner should ever initiate any discussion of the subject with anyone outside of the meeting except at the focus person's request.

A discernment group can meet virtually. For guidelines on virtual group discernment, go to www.listeninghearts.org/virtual.

Before the First Discernment Session with a Specific Focus Person

The guidelines below are designed for use by discernment groups in Listening Hearts training programs. Readers who will not be adopting these guidelines in a formal way may find portions that are helpful to their discernment.

1. A person who wishes to explore an issue or a sense of call notifies the contact person (a good listener who is well acquainted with the program and agrees to fill that role for a given community).

2. If at all feasible, the contact person meets with the potential focus person in person to explain how a discernment group works and to make sure that this prayerful approach is what the person is seeking. If an in-person meeting is not realistic, a phone conversation is a possibility. If the person chooses to continue, the contact person gives the focus person a copy of the 30th anniversary edition of *Listening Hearts* to

read (at least the first seven chapters and appendices 1 and 2).

3. In consultation with the focus person, the contact person recruits three persons from the pool of discerners to serve in the group, designating one of them to be the *convener*.

4. The convener makes all of the arrangements for the meeting, consulting with the focus person to choose a convenient comfortable location with a maximum of privacy and free from interruption. The convener opens and concludes the session, keeps track of the time, and makes sure that the transitions happen on time. But everyone, including the focus person, helps the group abide by the guidelines. Anyone can request that the pace slow down, request a period of silence, or request a break if the group has not yet taken one.

5. Three hours should be set aside for each meeting to ensure that no one will have to leave prematurely. Add ten minutes to fill out feedback forms, which are important for measuring the quality of the discernment process and making any needed improvements in the future. To make copies of feedback forms for a discernment session, go to www.listeninghearts.org/feedback.

6. In preparation for the first meeting, the focus person writes a brief sketch of not more than one typed page or three pages handwritten. **The focus person write-up needs to begin with a single, prayerfully conceived open-ended question addressed to God.** After that it traces significant threads of background and experience that relate to

the situation. When finished, the focus person either gives three copies to the convener to distribute or e-mails the convener a copy to distribute electronically.

7. A few days before the meeting, members of the group read the sketch and keep the focus person and the other discerners in their prayers. Praying in preparation for the meeting is of utmost importance.

8. To reinforce familiarity with the fundamentals, it is important that every member of the group review **chapters 1 through 7 and appendices 1 and 2 of *Listening Hearts*** in preparation for each discernment session. Since the intent of discernment is to develop a clear sense of what God may be saying, it is particularly important to study chapter 5, "**Is It God We Are Hearing**?" Also, review A Primer on Spiritual Discernment, especially topic 8, "Signs of the Spirit" at www.listeninghearts.org/signs.

9. The group should always meet as a whole, including the focus person. No discussions should take place outside the presence of the focus person.

10. If a member is unable to attend a scheduled meeting, the meeting should be rescheduled as soon as possible. If one member of the group needs to withdraw permanently from the commitment, the group may choose to replace that person and have a special meeting to bring the new member up to date.

11. Everyone should come to meetings prepared to schedule a time for another meeting, which means "bring your appointment calendar."

At the First Discernment Session

1. The convener arrives at the meeting place well before the starting time to arrange the chairs in an intimate circle—close enough for ease of listening and preferably equidistant from each other with each person able to see the others. A lighted candle, flowers, or an evocative piece of art at the center can help create a soothing atmosphere. When the focus person arrives, it is hospitable for everyone present to be standing to greet the focus person. The convener offers the focus person a choice of the chairs in the circle.

2. When the group assembles, if all do not know one another, the convener invites the discerners to introduce themselves with a few words about themselves before formally beginning the discernment session.

3. The convener opens the meeting with some words to help the focus person relax, then perhaps reads a suitable excerpt from scripture or offers an appropriate quotation to set the tone. Next, the convener offers an opening prayer, perhaps the adapted Thomas Merton Prayer on the last page of *Listening Hearts*. Then, to permit time for all to become receptive to God's presence, the convener announces a period of silence, specifying the amount of time, usually ten minutes, but possibly as little as two or three minutes if the focus person is unaccustomed to silence or uncomfortable with it. Before the

silence begins, the group may dim the lights to create a more reflective atmosphere.

4. The convener ends the silence by inviting the focus person to restate the question or issue for discernment and give a short summary of background information. As the focus person's comments conclude, the discerners may inquire about his or her interests, hobbies, and favorite ways to spend free time. (Later in the session, when the time for contemplative questions arrives, knowing this type of thing about the focus person will help the group come up with evocative questions appropriate to the particular focus person.)

5. The task of the members of the group is to **listen prayerfully and raise questions** that will help the focus person consider the issue in ways that bring new perspective. The questions need to be both caring and probing, designed to help the person move toward clearness and a deeper comprehension of the issue in relation to the path forward. See "Types of Discernment Questions" in appendix 2.

6. If the issue being considered is unclear, the first questions must deal with that. **It is crucial that everyone fully comprehends the question.** If the focus person presents multiple questions or issues, ask the focus person to identify a single question so that all present are concentrating on the same one. The other questions may fall away while the central question is being addressed, or the questions may need to be considered one at a time.

7. Next, **questions to establish relevant background** are in order. These questions toward the

beginning of the session deal with background information: circumstances of the situation, the cast of characters, the context. After that, it can be fruitful to identify and weigh options, then consider known impediments to implementing them. **Then, the pace of the questions slows down. The questions become more reflective. More space is left between the focus person's response and the next question. Slowly, the reflective questions become more evocative, tapping into the unconscious . . .** and the pace gets even slower.

8. Keep the questions concise and present them one at a time. **Do not explain the reason for any question.**

9. If you are unsure exactly how to phrase a question, it is better to wait silently to give the question time to develop and come into clearer focus. If you need time, request a period of silence. **The person requesting the silence is the one to break the silence.**

10. The background information supplied by the focus person is often fertile soil for questions. How a person has experienced call in the past can be a guide to hearing a call now. What is "between the lines" is often as important as what is written. Careful, caring inquiry can draw out the unsaid. Avoid questions like "What does God want you to do?" If the person knew the answer, the group would not be gathered for discernment.

11. Ultimately, the **purpose of the questions is to elicit signs of call.** For this reason, imaginative, intui-

tive questions can be fruitful, even though they may seem "off the wall."

12. Questions designed to call forth scripture passages and images can bear rich fruit for a person well acquainted with the Bible.

13. Discerners must **refrain from giving advice.** Do not ask questions that suggest the answer or cloak advice in the guise of questions. Do not ask questions that stem from curiosity alone.

14. It is advisable for the focus person to keep the responses brief because more questions and more silence may provide further clarity. A certain amount of wandering can lead to helpful discoveries; yet if the focus person strays far off course or keeps repeating things, someone in the group needs to intervene. To do so, wait for a pause or request a moment of silence. Then pose a question about a particular point that the focus person seems to be trying to make.

15. While articulating answers to the questions is usually helpful, **the focus person is never obligated to answer any question.** If a question is truly from God, it will plant itself deep within until the focus person is ready to ponder it at some future time.

16. The work of God often takes place in the depth of quiet. It is important that each person be conscious of permitting **a period of prayerful silence between speakers**.

17. Each member of the group needs to help maintain a pace that allows for reflection. Any member of the group, including the focus person, can ask that the cadence of questions slow down or that questions stop altogether for a few minutes of silence. **The**

person requesting the silence is the one to break the silence.

18. Each member of the group needs to help maintain a gentle atmosphere, guarding against any tendency to become confrontational. This does not mean to avoid asking hard questions. Confrontational questions arise when the questioner wants a given answer or presumes to know what is best for the person. Such questions tend to be expressed with feelings of anger. **A good discerner raises questions with a humble and listening heart but is willing to ask difficult questions.**

19. Truly open listening in a group is hard and yet it is essential to the process. Avoid formulating questions in your mind while someone else is speaking. Let your questions develop during the silence between questions. If you need time to let a question congeal, you may request a period of silence.

20. Each member of the group must help ensure that members do not press their own agendas or feelings on the focus person. **A discernment session is not about solving a problem**. It is an occasion to (1) discover signs of the Spirit in the person's past that led up to the matter being considered, (2) see what God might be trying to say through the present situation, and (3) develop a sense of where the Spirit is pointing.

21. Each member of the group should try to make sure that there is adequate silence so that every discerner has sufficient opportunity to ask questions.

22. During the meeting, members of the group can test whether they are really listening to one another

by keeping in mind these two questions: Do I have an open mind with respect to the issues being considered? Is anything keeping me from really listening to one of the persons present?

23. The session usually takes the full three hours. A break at about the midpoint is recommended. The group can determine whether the break will be silent or talking. Following the break, it is helpful to take a few minutes of silence to become centered once again, after which the convener can invite the group to pick up where it left off.

24. In the course of a discernment session, various threads emerge. Toward the end of the session, it is helpful to raise questions that help **draw these threads together**.

25. About thirty minutes before the anticipated end of the meeting, the convener begins to look for an opening to switch gears and offer the focus person an opportunity to ask something of the group. Perhaps the focus person will ask to hear experiences the discerners have had that offer parallels. Or the focus person may prefer a period of silence. **This is the time for the focus person to do the asking and for the group to respond.**

26. On occasion, a focus person has requested that each member of the group take a turn inviting a prayer image. To do this, each discerner, one at a time, stands behind the focus person with hands on the head of the focus person. In silence and with eyes closed, the discerner holds the focus person in prayer, awaiting a "picture" that may bring insight to the unfolding situation. The discerner describes the

image in as much detail as possible without offering an interpretation. This exercise has produced some vivid perceptions. Any discerner for whom a picture does not arise may offer a prayer or simply say "Amen."

27. About ten minutes before the end of the session, the convener asks the group to determine whether or not another meeting is desirable. Sometimes another meeting is useful, if only to give everyone time to reflect and pray, in which case new insights may arise. If anyone in the group is not fully at peace with the direction in which the focus person seems to be moving, it is exceedingly important for that person to suggest that the group convene again. Do not state the reason. Everyone needs to keep in mind the importance of **spiritual consensus** in this process. **If no one thinks that there is need for another meeting, this signals that everyone feels that the signs of the Spirit are strong enough to confirm that the focus person is moving in the right direction.** Thus, spiritual consensus has been reached. If another meeting is not planned, the convener should make it clear that the focus person can request another meeting at a later time by contacting the convener.

28. The final five minutes are for free and open prayers, which the convener introduces and concludes.

29. **At any time during the meeting, a sense that the group has crossed a threshold may emerge.** A member may suggest that a common understanding seems to exist. Should this occur, the convener

may check out this perception with the group and, if verified, move on to the final thirty minutes of the meeting as laid out in guideline #25.

30. Discernment sessions are occasions for "quickening"—the first stirring of insight or understanding of a way forward, though not necessarily with immediate resolution. Discernment often continues to unfold after discernment sessions have concluded. The consensus may be that the group has gone as far as it can for the time being. Should this occur, the desire to "wrap things up" neatly or to come to closure on a particular question should be resisted. Later events, choices, or circumstances may become the place where God brings to fruition the work that has been done. **Neither the planting nor the harvest belongs to us**. Thus, at the time the meeting concludes, it is wise to avoid summary advice or comment so that we do not reap before the time of the harvest.

31. At the end of every discernment session, the convener distributes feedback forms to be filled out and handed in before leaving.

32. The convener gives the completed feedback forms to the contact person who monitors the implementation of the program.

33. Before leaving, discerners return their copies of the focus person write-up to the focus person. Or, if it was distributed electronically, they delete it.

34. Prayer and discernment continue after the group disperses. Any member of the group may subsequently develop a strong sense that it would be beneficial to reconvene, in which case that person

may call the convener and suggest another meeting. The convener would then call the focus person to see if the focus person is open to the group coming back together again. And of course, the focus person is always at liberty to initiate the group's gathering again by notifying the convener.

Reminders for the Discerners

• Remember that first and foremost, you are gathered in prayer. Be attuned to one another and to the Holy Spirit.

• Discernment is a fluid process. The focus person comes with a question based on one or more concerns. Quite often, the question will evolve, and the initial problems recede. Try to make sure that the original issue has truly been resolved. Otherwise, the focus person may leave feeling serene but wake up the next morning experiencing the turmoil of the problem anew.

• Avoid functioning as three individuals charting separate paths. Instead, become attuned to the Holy Spirit flowing through one another so that you can be drawn forward as one body. Build on the questions of others. Be attentive to the way the person responds—not only what is said, but also the timing, tone of voice, facial expressions, and body language.

• Do not simply follow where the focus person leads. Continually remind yourself that you are following the Holy Spirit.

• Do not store up your questions. **Listen, listen, listen**. Let the Holy Spirit determine if and when the opportunity comes to raise the questions that occur to you.

• In a discernment session, a focus person sometimes becomes strongly drawn to one particular thing: a scripture passage, a dream, a memory, an analogy, certain words, a particular question, or a visual image. This may be a key to unlock a door. **If the discerners explore and probe possible associations, the right questions may arise, and the door may open.**

• When you detect **energy** in a person's response, it is a sign of the Spirit. Take note and look for follow-up questions.

• Sometimes a person feels a strong sense of call but does not seem to be able to follow it. This person may seek discernment to find out what stands in the way of living out a call. In such a situation, it may be important to consider the possibility that the call may be authentic, but some aspect of the call may not be properly understood. A **genuine call usually produces the energy to fulfill it.**

• On the one hand, discernment needs to be expansive and imaginative, opening up the doors to possibilities beyond our desires or expectations. On the other hand, discerners must stay in touch with the practical realities of the situation. In the course of any session, it is advisable to **explore both ends of the spectrum.**

• **Honor the focus person's responses in silence.** If the focus person's response goes unusually deep or strikes a profound emotional chord, leave extra time for the impact to penetrate before raising another question.

• If the group seems to be grasping for questions, it probably indicates that the questions are coming from the head. This is a good time for someone to ask for a period of silence so that the group can become more centered and unified, more confident that God will provide. **The best discernment questions usually quietly bubble up from deep down.** It is the quality of the questions, not the quantity or frequency, that bring forth spiritual discernment.

• In the course of a discernment session, it may become apparent that the issues that are emerging go beyond what discerners are trained to address—issues that may be deeply difficult, emotionally, psychologically, or otherwise. Should that occur, it is appropriate to draw the meeting to a conclusion, gently. The convener may say, "I think that we have gone as far as we can for the moment. Perhaps we should let matters rest and possibly get together again at a later date."

• On the rare occasion that discerners may encounter a serious problem in terms of how they dealt with a discernment session, they may need to meet without the focus person to address their own handling of the situation. At such a meeting, it is crucial that **the discerners discuss procedures only** and make no reference to the content of the discernment issue. It is also paramount that they do nothing to cast blame on the focus person but look only at how they might have worked together more constructively.

• **Be mindful of signs of the Spirit**. It is important to distinguish between pleasant feelings of serenity and the peace of God, which presents itself as a strong sense of confidence and well-being arising from deep within—often welling up from beneath the turbulence of a difficult situation. As the discernment approaches what seems to be its end, it is crucial that each member of the group share a true sense of God's peace. Any member who feels any sense of agitation or disquiet needs to make it known so that the discernment continues until the peace of God envelops the entire gathering, bringing forth true spiritual consensus.

• In the final segment of the meeting, if the focus person asks the members of the group to share their own experiences, do not present your experience in a way that gives advice. Your experience can speak for itself; the focus person can glean from it what is helpful. Limit your response to what the focus person has asked of you.

Appendix 2
Types of Discernment Questions

The words "question" and "quest" come from the same Latin root, *quaerere*, which means "to search or seek." This is the context in which we use questions for discernment: not to interrogate but to explore—looking for signs that point the way for us. Thomas Merton offered testimony to the value of well-conceived questions when he wrote the following of his professor at Columbia, Mark Van Doren:

> *Most of the time he asked questions. His questions were very good, and if you tried to answer them intelligently, you found yourself saying things that you did not know you knew, and that you had not, in fact, known before. He had "educed" them from you by his question. Do not think that Mark was simply priming his students with thoughts of his own, and then making the thought stick to their minds by getting them to give it back to him as their own. . . . The results were sometimes quite unexpected . . . casting lights that he had not himself foreseen.*[2]

There is a flow and sequence to questions in a Listening Hearts discernment session. It begins with questions to establish clarity in regard to the discernment question and the background information. It moves into a slower, more reflective phase and eventually to a contemplative phase in which profound silence gives rise to evocative questions to spark metaphors or images. Then, at the appropriate time, the discerners move into questions that draw the threads together.

Rational Questions

(to nail down the basic information)

Here are samples of the kinds of questions a discerner might consider at the onset of exploring a call. They are not for repeating verbatim, but for stimulating questions that uniquely speak to the particular person and the situation under consideration.

- What options exist?
- Are there impediments to implementing them?
- What are the advantages?
- What are the disadvantages?
- Are there any risks involved?
- Can you afford it?
- What impact will it have on your family? How will your spouse (or colleagues or children or parents or friends) feel about it?
- What strengths do you bring to it? What weaknesses?
- Do you have any commitments that will be affected?

• Are you overworked? Too busy? Not busy enough?

• Is this something you have thought about doing for a long time? Is now the time? How do you know? Are you feeling rushed to make a decision?

• What people have influenced your thinking on this?

• Do you feel obligated to do this?

• Might a desire for approval be influencing you?

• How concerned are you about your reputation?

• What are the needs of the community? What do those needs suggest to you?

If you are not sure that you have an adequate grasp of the basic information, do not let the group move on to the reflective questions. Request some silence to give yourself time to formulate any additional questions you need to ask.

Once you leave the informational/rational questions, do not revert to them. You are moving to a deeper level. If you return to asking informational questions, you will exit the zone you were operating in and it will be difficult to reenter it.

Reflective Questions

(to release the facts into the imagination)

Reflective questions move the discerner and/or the group downward to the level of the physical heart, which is the level of the semiconscious, a meditative level. The entire group needs to be immersed in the Spirit and attuned to one another so that they move in unison. It is a matter of taking what has transpired at the rational level and setting it free to roam. Reflective questions help the focus person:

(a) reflect on his or her motives,
(b) get in touch with desires and fears,
(c) explore when and how God has worked in his or her life over the years,
(d) notice how things have unfolded in previous situations that have similarities, and
(e) imagine possibilities for the future.

Reflective questions serve as a bridge from the mind to the heart. Examples include:

- If you could go somewhere else and simply leave behind the burdens of your current situation, what might you lose?
- Imagine yourself relaxed—floating on a cloud—viewing your predicament from above, what would it look like?
- How do you imagine your life unfolding if you take this action? What are the likely gains? What might you lose?
- Imagine that you simply ignore the situation and let life go on, what are things likely to look like as the years roll on?
- Imagine yourself in a rudderless boat. Where do you see life taking you?
- If you were the other person in this situation, how do you think you would feel? What do you think you might do?

Evocative Questions

(to elicit images from the focus person's center)

Evocative questions help a person uncover thoughts and feelings that are below the surface. Emotions can be very complex. When you ask people how they feel, usually they can mention only the emotions that are closest to the surface. It is better to help them find metaphors that can uncover a wide range of thoughts, feelings, and memories that are buried in their unconscious. Things they know, but do not know that they know. For this purpose, **evocative questions that call forth images tend to be more fruitful than overt questions**. Analogies sparked by drawing upon a person's areas of interest (sports, business, finance, family, nature) can be explored to reveal God's presence. The group can invite associations with scripture, art, music, literature, or science as a way of bringing signs of the Spirit to light. Visual images and recalling the sounds of music, nature, or a raucous party can bring back long forgotten memories.

Discerners need to resist the temptation of suggesting their own images to the focus person. It is infinitely better to help the focus person access his or her own images. As a discerner, try to let the ideas and images that come to you increase your own understanding, which in turn can help you pose questions that enable the focus person to hit upon their own analogies, metaphors, or scripture references. The aim of evocative questions is to take the focus person to the center of their being. The questions need to emanate from deep within the discerners.

Below are some examples of the kinds of questions you might ask:

• As you think about your situation, is there a person in the Bible with whom you identify?

• Does any theme or passage from scripture occur to you as you wrestle with this?

• What colors would you select to express your feelings at this moment?

• *If the focus person is interested in sports:* How do athletes approach this kind of challenge? *or* Can you draw an analogy with any athletic endeavor?

• *To a person who is an avid reader:* Do you feel like a character in any book you have read?

• To *a music lover:* As you envision taking that path, what kind of music do you hear playing?

• *To a person who is interested in the theater:* Does any play come to mind as you consider the issue?

• *To a weaver or person who enjoys sewing:* Can you describe the fabric that might convey this situation? How would you be likely to use it?

• *If the focus person speaks of running into a wall:* What is the wall made of? How high is it? How thick? (Then explore the properties of whatever materials constitute the wall.) How might you go over, through, or around it? What is on the other side?

• *If the focus person refers to a door:* Is the door open or closed? What happens if you step through the doorway? What do you see? Can you smell anything?

What does it feel like in there? What happens if you do not go through?

• *If the focus person refers to a road:* Do you recognize this road? Are you alone on the road? What does it look like? Is it light out or is it dark? Are you walking? Driving? Can you see what is ahead? What is on either side? Are you comfortable on this road? Do you wish you could get off it? Do you see an exit? Is it open or blocked? Is there a sign that tells where it takes you? How do you feel about taking it?

Integrative Questions

(to draw the threads together)

As the session moves toward a close, begin to raise questions that help connect the various strands that have emerged in the course of the session.

Always keep in mind that it is important that all members of a discernment group be attuned to the sequence of questions and to each other so that the group moves together as one. If the group is moving to the next step before you, as a discerner or a focus person, are ready, request a period of silence to provide time to sit quietly with what has been developing. **The person requesting the silence is the one to break the silence.**

> *If I had an hour to solve a problem and my life depended on it, I would use the first 55 minutes determining the proper questions to ask.*
>
> —Albert Einstein

Appendix 3
Informal History of the Project and the Research Methods Used

by Suzanne Farnham

The ideas that eventually developed into this book began to percolate in April 1987 at Kirkridge Retreat and Study Center in Bangor, Pennsylvania, at a conference, "Solitude and Community." Parker Palmer, one of the conference leaders, spoke at length about the Quakers and set up small groups to meet in the evenings and function as Quaker "clearness committees." In a Friends Meeting, a person who is wrestling with a personal decision can ask for a clearness committee—a small group of people to meet with and help the person develop a sense of direction.

As one who has constantly wrestled with personal questions of vocation, I volunteered to be a "focus person." Parker distributed some guidelines. We dived in. Most of the people at the conference were Protestant clergy with backgrounds strong in pastoral counseling and weak in contemplation. They found it difficult to abide by guidelines requiring Quaker silence and not giving advice. Even so, the process proved helpful, and I experienced an increased sense of clarity. It seemed to be a method worth taking back to my parish.

At the same conference, I struck up a conversation with Jan Hoffman, who, at that time, was Clerk of the New England Yearly Meeting of Friends. When she heard I was from Baltimore, she mentioned that the Baltimore Friends were known and respected nationwide. I had not known this and began to think it would be good to capitalize on such a resource.

Upon returning home, I began to consider making a little study: reading a few books, interviewing a few Quakers, and attending some Friends Meetings.

Things soon began to snowball. I started to feel that the Quakers had a highly effective process but did not sufficiently use some of the tests of discernment employed by others. My thought was to integrate the two.

For several years I had been looking for a concise compilation of principles for discernment that went beyond the Ignatian Rules, but to no avail. My spiritual director, Patricia Scanlan, then prioress of the Baltimore Carmel, suggested that all of the spiritual classics were laced with information on discernment of call, although not necessarily using those terms. With help from Mother Virginia of the All Saints Convent, Barbara Platt, who is theologically trained and at the time served as executive director of the Stoney Run Friends in Baltimore, and Bill Rich, who then headed the deacons' formation program for the Diocese of Maryland, I put together a bibliography. The list was too long for me to handle alone, so I began to recruit people to help with the reading. The vestry of Memorial Church pledged to support the work. The Committee on the Ministry of the Laity of the Diocese of Maryland gave $500 to purchase the books. Bishop Eastman provided a grant for new initiatives. The Christian Vocation Research Project was under way.

I bought books, purchased hi-liters and colored pens, and made out an instruction sheet. Each volunteer was to read an assigned book, marking the portions of the book containing information on call, discernment, or community according to a color-coded scheme. They were also invited to make comments in the margins and to write summaries when the material was implicit or diffuse. It took forty people to do this reading, which included over one hundred titles.

Another problem arose: the amount of information gathered was overwhelming. As a solution, I recruited five of the readers to help sift through the material, organize and evaluate it, design a discernment program for use in parishes, and put together a handbook. Naively, I said that we would meet for an hour and a half every week for three months. In fact, we met almost every week for over two years; some of the meetings lasted all day.

One of the five, Andy Barasda, was between jobs and had offered to help us get started but had said that he might not be able to continue for the full three months. He put in five months before retiring. A second member of the group, Jenny Ramberg, met with us weekly for the first nine months. Her sudden and untimely death dealt a big loss because of her personal warmth as well as her scholarship in feminist theology. This left us with the group of four— Joe, Teto, Sue, and me—who met weekly for another year and a half and eventually came to realize that we were writing a book, not just a handbook.

Before the original group of six met, Joe volunteered to take notes of the meetings, enter them on his computer, and print and distribute them to the group for review and reflection. This offer turned out to be crucial to the development of the project. After our very first meeting, I realized that it was going to be very difficult to keep track of all the data. I asked Joe if he could extract the pieces of information from the minutes and catalog them according to category. He asked me to come up with subdivisions. I identified eight questions that we were trying to answer; these became the titles for our eight working papers. From that point on, as each of us went through the books that had been read and marked, we wrote down relevant information, indicating which working paper it was to go on, and gave it to Joe. Every entry was numbered and entered as a separate item on one of the eight working papers. Since these papers were fluid, we dated each edition. These were the foundation for our work when we gathered.

Every meeting began with ten minutes of silence. When the need for further silence arose in the course of a meeting, we either fell into it naturally or someone requested it. We worked through all of the information using spiritual consensus. Each idea from the working papers was considered until everyone agreed what to do with it: integrate it into a preliminary draft that we called a "narrative," include it in a note, or drop it. The titles of the narratives corresponded to the titles of the working papers. Joe worked our decisions into the narratives—not a small task! Then, as the narratives were refined, they became drafts of chapters 1 through 7 or appendices 1 and 2.

The following sample from one page of one working paper from a specific date helps to illustrate the process:

How Can We Evaluate If It Is God We Are Hearing?

Where to Look

54. "In order to discern we need to learn how to read our own history, to see the turning points, the movements of change, the unfolding of God's plan for us at each new step of the way." (de Waal, p. 73.)

56. Christ addresses me in the voice of each person I meet. (de Waal, p. 126.)

63. Discover what you believe and value by observing what you do. (Kelsey & Haldane.)

64. Examine your ideas against the opposite ideas.

66. Some thoughts come through direct inspiration, some through God's friends, some through creatures or objects.

85. When trying to tap the full potential of any nucleus of human energy, you need to tap into those qualities within it which are unique and incommunicable. (de Chardin, *Building the Earth.*)

104. John the Baptist's disciples complained to him that the people were now being baptized by Jesus, the person to whom John had borne witness. John

replied, “A person can lay claim only to what is given him from heaven.”

115. The poor are too often left to God. Therefore, forget those who are better placed and remember the poor. (Fox/Eckhart.)

121. There are stories from our lives through which God is trying to tell us things we need to know. We need to identify those stories, tell them, and try to sort them out. (Multiple sources.)

124. Discover what you believe and value by observing what you do. (Multiple sources.)

128. What the god does is more important than the words people say. (Egyptian Book of Amen, as related in *Proclamation Commentaries: Genesis, Exodus, Leviticus, Numbers*, Foster R. McCurley, Ed.)

Some entries were rearranged, so that the numbers were not necessarily in sequence. As entries were processed and integrated into the narratives, they dropped out of the working papers.

In preparation for each meeting, members of the group handed in new entries, Joe updated the working papers and narratives and eventually the chapters we would be using, and I made copies and distributed them to the others ahead of time.

At the same time, a separate area of inquiry was also under way. In the early stages of thinking about this project, Fred Wolf, who was then Bishop of Maine, suggested that it was important that any work on discernment of call address the issues of support for ministry and accountability. To investigate these areas of concern, another group of people set about gathering information. Each person took responsibility for studying a different group: the Quakers, the Lutherans, the Episcopal Diocese of Central New York, the rural parishes in the Episcopal Diocese of Delaware, the Sojourners, the Church of the Saviour in Washington, D.C., and the Kittamaqundi Community in Columbia, Maryland. They interviewed people, made visitations, did reading and then synthesized their findings by coming together for discussion on three Saturdays. Those who saw this portion of the research effort through to completion were Barbara Cates, Jeff Eller, Barney Farnham, Pam Fleming, Caroline Naylor, and Dick Roszel. The fruits of this research became chapters 8 and 9.

The copy editor, authors, and theologians who read through the various drafts of the manuscript and made suggestions became our teachers, our mentors.

As the guidelines for discernment took shape, we developed a training program for discerners. We field-tested the book, the training program, and the discernment group, all with the help of our consultant, Russell Ayers.

We then incorporated as a nonprofit organization for the purpose of implementing our programs and continuing the research. The bylaws of the corporation stipulate that all meetings of the trustees and of any committees be conducted incorporating silence and arriving at decisions through spiritual consensus.

Writing this book was itself an experience in Christian community that touched our lives deeply.

Appendix 4
Cultivating a Discerning Community

You can read about a foreign country and thereby get an introduction to life in that place and a foundation for understanding its culture. After that, a visit can give you a bit of a feel for that culture. But to assimilate the culture, you have to move there and live among its people for a period of time.

Spiritual discernment is like that: it runs counter to the culture in which we live. Reading about discernment is an important first step to learning about it. But to internalize the culture of spiritual discernment, you have to spend time in it. Listening Hearts programs offer the opportunity to experience this culture. Programs are offered primarily to communities of faith such as congregations, seeker groups, governing boards, clergy groups, schools, and dioceses/judicatories. Each program is held at a location agreed upon by the sponsoring group and Listening Hearts.

Listening Hearts Retreats and Workshops afford a setting and structure for participants to engage in spiritual discernment around their own life situations. Silence, song, creative meditation activities, and sharing of reflections weave together to draw people closer to God and one another as they gain direction for their lives. These programs give members of a group an avenue to seek God's guidance about the personal or professional issues they face and bring them together in a way that builds Christian community. These retreats are suitable for congregations, groups of seekers, student groups, diocesan/judicatory gatherings, clergy groups, or conference center programs. Each retreat is custom designed to meet the needs of the specific group. They can range in length from a few hours to a full weekend.

Grounded in God Retreats teach decision-making groups how to work through their issues using deep listening, prayerful speaking, creative engagement with scripture, and spiritual consensus. Groups that commit to this approach find that deliberative bodies can have meetings that are energizing and spiritually nourishing. When seeking spiritual consensus, controversial issues can actually draw members closer to God and one another. These retreats experientially teach vestries, church boards, search committees, planning teams, and other deliberative groups how to work through controversial issues in a way that strengthens spiritual community. For a congregation, organization, or governing board that finds itself severely divided by a controversial issue, there is a retreat for spiritual conflict resolution.

Training Programs for Trainers are for spiritually mature leaders who want to spread the practice of spiritual discernment. Participants go through the program they plan to teach, learn the underlying principles and rationale of the program, and receive virtual master copies of the computer-generated materials they will need when they lead the programs.

For detailed information about Listening Hearts programs, publications, and resource materials, go to www.listeninghearts.org.

Notes

Acknowledgments

1. Hammarskjöld, p. 89.

Introduction

1. Rilke, pp. 34–35 (emphasis in original).
2. Kierkegaard, pp. 4–5 (emphasis in original).
3. Meaningful coincidences known as synchronicity and becoming one with our lives through flow lead to the conclusion that the cosmos "responds to our actions," writes Nelson-Isaacs, p. 194. This is because we "can't separate the answers we get from the questions we ask to obtain them" (Ibid., p. 11). Rovelli, p. 17, notes that electrons—elementary particles found in all atoms—"only exist when someone or something watches them, or better, when they are interacting with something else." Does this mean that "reality is only interaction"? (Ibid., p. 18). Phillips, p. 106, writes, "We can no longer consider objects as independently existing entities. They are interconnected in ways not even conceivable in classical physics." See also Schroeder, p. 151 ("Existence is closer to being an association of ideas than a conglomeration of atoms.").
4. Attributed to Bhagawan Nityananda, Indian Guru (1897–1961)

Chapter 1. What Is "Call"?

1. ***Call*** can be used interchangeably with the word ***vocation,*** which comes from the Latin word ***vocare,*** "to call." ***Vocation,*** however, often has a broad connotation, while ***call*** may refer to something more specific. A person might have a vocation as a choral director, for example, and a call to work with a specific chorus at a particular time.
2. See Luther, p. 311. Luther compares the call of a priest or monk to the call of a farmer laboring in the field or a woman looking after her home. See also de Waal, p. 117. De Waal writes that the Rule of St. Benedict, which sets forth the aims and practices of the Benedictine monastic life, "totally cuts through the sham that any one person is superior to any other or could have more value than any other."
3. Compare Luther, p. 311.
4. Futrell, ***Ignatian Discernment,*** p. 49; see also de Waal, p. 153.
5. Futrell, ***Ignatian Discernment,*** p. 49.
6. de Waal, p. 153. To think of God as outside the places or circumstances of our own life can prevent us from hearing God's call. Buber, p. 74, put it this way:

> Creation is not a hurdle on the road to God; it is the road itself. We are created along with one another and directed to a life with one another. Creatures are placed in my way so that I, their fellow creature, by means of them and with them, may find the way to God. A God reached by excluding them would not be the God of all beings in whom all being is fulfilled.

Buber wrote this in disagreement with Sören Kierkegaard (quoted in Buber, p. 74), who had renounced his relationship with Regina Olsen, saying, "In order to come to love, I had to remove the object."

7. Compare Orsy, pp. 160–61.
8. McNeill, Morrisson, and Nouwen, p. 83. While the authors discuss only the distinction between vocation and career, not everyone has a job that is also a career. Yet there is an equally valid distinction between vocation and occupation, i.e., one's livelihood, whether or not it is a career. Work, of itself, may or may not be vocation. Undue emphasis on work of any kind can leave little time, place, or room for God's call. See de Waal, p. 107: "There is no nonsense here about it being in some way praiseworthy to be overworked."

   On the other hand, as our lives become more centered in God, we tend to grow in our sense that God touches others through our work, whatever that work may be. When we go into the workplace, we carry Christ with us. See Brother Lawrence, throughout.

   Ordained ministers can be particularly susceptible to regarding their priestly occupations as synonymous with God's call. Ordained ministers also have responsibilities toward family, friends, and self. To ignore such responsiblities and devote time excessively to matters of ordained ministry can deafen even a priestly ear to God's entire call. Thus, C. S. Lewis cautioned Sheldon Vanauken against becoming a priest because it could debase his Christianity by turning it into an occupation. Vanauken, pp. 105–6.
9. Compare Burtness, p. 92.

10. "Are we to understand the 'imitation of Christ' in the sense that we should copy his life," asks Carl G. Jung, "or in the deeper sense that we are to live our own proper lives as truly as he lived his in its individual uniqueness?" Jung answers his own question: "It is no easy matter to live a life that is modelled on Christ's, but it is unspeakably harder to live one's own life as truly as Christ lived his." Jung, p. 340.
11. Futrell, ***Ignatian Discernment,*** p. 54. Compare Merton, ***New Seeds,*** p. 32. Merton writes, "Our vocation is not simply to ***be,*** but to work together with God in the creation of our own life, our own identity, our own destiny." See also Merton, ***Seven Storey Mountain,*** p. 130.
12. L'Engle, p. 27.
13. Green, pp. 139–40. Green sees the devil testing us by false "consolation," an apparent, though mistaken, feeling of spiritual peace that locks us in place and prevents us from moving forward in greater service to the Lord. Barclay, pp. 267–68, discusses the parable of the wedding feast, pointing out that the things that make people deaf to God's call are not necessarily bad in themselves:

> One man went to his estate, the other to his business. They did not go off on a wild carousal or an immoral adventure. They went off on the, in itself, excellent task of efficiently administering their business life. . . . The tragedy of life is that it is so often the second bests which shut out the bests, that it is things which are good in themselves which shut out the things that are supreme.

14. Compare Green, p. 99: "Discernment is where prayer meets action." See James 2:17: "So faith by itself, if it has no works, is dead." See also de Waal, p. 78: "We get there by deeds, not words."
15. Compare de Waal, p. 17: "Genuine fruitfulness comes from what at first seems sterile."
16. The image of fruit seems particularly apt when describing the results of responding to God's call. It may take many years before a seed becomes a tree. Even after the tree is grown, it may be a long time before it produces fruit and still longer before the fruit ripens. It is a mistake to look for immediate results after responding to God's call. Such a stance can encourage people to manufacture forced or artificial fruit, as if to "prove" a call from God. Nevertheless, it is well for us to consider the possibility that if we do not bear fruit, we may be gathered up and burned (John 15:6).
17. McNeill, Morrison, and Nouwen, p. 36.
18. McNeill, Morrison, and Nouwen, p. 40. See also p. 36: "Obedience is hearing God's loving word and responding to it." Compare de Waal, p. 43: ". . . to obey really means to hear and then act upon what we have heard."
19. de Waal, p. 49.
20. Servant Leadership School Program Offerings, p. 2.
21. Ulanov and Ulanov, p. 9.

Chapter 2. Call to Ministry

1. Fenhagen, ***Mutual Ministry,*** p. 21.
2. ***The Book of Common Prayer,*** p. 855 (from the "Catechism").

3. Compare Sedgwick, p. 6: ". . . when ministry focuses on the image of service alone then specific acts of service become ends in themselves."
4. Williams, p. 193.

Chapter 3. What Is Discernment?

1. Futrell, ***Ignatian Discernment,*** p. 47. Futrell discusses the Ignatian concept of ***diakrisis pneumaton,*** "discernment of Spirits."
2. As with all gifts from God, there is no way to compel the gift of discernment. Compare Green, p. 116: "There are no techniques for producing the experience of God."
3. Diocese of Bethlehem, p. 1.
4. Compare Ignatius of Loyola, pp. 129–34, "Rules for the Discernment of Spirits." Even these rules, which are for perceiving and understanding "to some degree" the different movements produced in the soul, are not so much rules as they are an outline of peaks (consolations) and valleys (desolations) on a spiritual landscape.
5. Sheeran, pp. 24–25.
6. Sheeran, p. 24.
7. Sheeran, p. 25, quoting Vernon Noble.
8. Sheeran, p. 25. Another test used by the early Quakers was a person's own "inner leadings." Yet as Sheeran points out (pp. 26, 28–29), in assessing those leadings the early Quakers failed to consider the writings on discernment that preceded them, such as those of Ignatius. Nor did they use any external benchmark to test such leadings.

Compare Johnston, ***The Still Point,*** p. 114. Johnston discusses G.K. Chesterton's distaste for what Chesterton called "Funny Interior Feeling." Chesterton (quoted in Johnston, p. 114) said, "When Jones obeys the inner light, Jones obeys Jones." Chesterton articulates Roman Catholic thinking from the time of the Reformation, which stresses reliance on external, ecclesiastical authority to guide conduct. Johnston is also wary of reliance on inner feelings alone. He suggests (pp. 114–16) that inner promptings can come from our own neuroses and that, since most people are not sufficiently developed spiritually, "a science of ethics and asceticism is necessary."

9. Futrell, ***Ignatian Discernment,*** p. 53.
10. The understanding that discernment takes place in a close relationship with the Lord may offer the best insight into how discernment occurs. Thinking of discernment as a process or an art may be helpful but also invites problems.

    Green, p. 57, states that discernment is "the art of finding God's will." This is useful as a contrast to merely applying rules or precepts that may frustrate discernment, but it can also be misleading. The essence of art is individual creativity. While the ability to discern also involves creativity, it occurs, not by individual effort alone, but through a relationship with the Lord. As Green, p. 64, also says:

    > The essential truth [is] that discernment is a function of a loving, personal relationship to the Lord. It can normally be only as deep and as solid as that relationship itself. The true discerner must be a praying, loving person.

Another word used to describe how discernment occurs is ***process.*** This word often strikes a chord with those who have a strong bent for the spiritual because they frequently perceive life, death, and resurrection as a continuing process.

"Process theology" takes the radical viewpoint that all of creation, including God, is dynamic and in the process of change. What is real is in process. Alfred North Whitehead is considered the father of the movement. Disciples embrace the writings of Pierre Teilhard de Chardin, Henri Bergeson, and William Temple. Some consider John Cobb's ***God and the World*** to be the best book on the subject.

For many, however, the word ***process*** means a step-by-step procedure that culminates in a specific result, like a chemical reaction. Scientists and lawyers are among those who may fall into this category. Because the word ***process*** has different associations among different people, it may be best not to emphasize it when speaking about discernment.

11. This does not mean that ***only*** those people who have an intimate relationship with God will be called by God or will be able to hear such a call. For example, Moses' relationship with God seemed to follow from, not precede, his call. Like Moses in his early life, many of us are in the beginning stages of our spiritual relationship with God, not yet close, not yet trusting, not having an intimate relationship—yet wanting to hear God's call. The call to Moses is a reminder that, despite our timidity, we can hear God's voice, even if it seems that a great gulf now separates us from God:

> . . . who [in the Bible] besides Jesus really knew which end was up? **Nobody.** Not Moses. Don't

tell me Moses. He was a nice man, and he kept in beautiful touch with his God, and all that—but that's exactly the point. He had to keep in touch. Jesus realized there ***is*** no separation from God (Salinger, p. 170; emphasis in original).

12. Orsy, p. 182, cautions against using the expression "finding the will of God," noting that "it would take volumes to explicate" its complexities. He explains (pp. 166–67):

    The expression "will of God" carries many meanings, numerous enough to trap the unwary. An attempt to analyze it immediately recalls subtle distinctions between God's positive will and his permissive will. It recalls also the bitter disputes between Dominicans and Jesuits who locked themselves for so long into the wrong question about divine initiative and human freedom. Our purpose here cannot be to undertake a full analysis of past subtleties. But past animosities should make us careful in using the expression. We should remember, too, that many saints did not have or need a scientifically elaborate concept to seek and to find God's will. Their pilgrimage to [God] did not depend on sophisticated theology.

13. See Orsy (p. 185): "For practical purposes the expression 'seeking and finding the will of God' should be taken as meaning 'to seek and find the next step in the service of the Lord.' "

    Green (p. 96) employs a similar concept in considering the meaning of the Ignatian rules for understanding "to some extent" the movements of the Spirit. The words ***to some extent*** are Ignatius' words. In Green's view, they are important because God "does not give us a total, long-range blueprint of his will" but rather "reveals his will to us step by step." Tilden Edwards, Episcopal priest, author, and founder of the Shalem Institute in Washington, D.C., suggests that discernment is not discovery of God's will, which "forever remains a mystery," but instead is "aligning ourselves" with God. (Interview, January 30, 1989.)

14. Diocese of Bethlehem, p. 2. Compare Polanyi, p. x: "Things which we can tell, we know by observing them; those that we cannot tell, we know by dwelling in them."
15. Diocese of Bethlehem, p. 2: "Although discernment involves understanding, it is very delicate and is easily clobbered by too much comprehension, or analytical knowledge."
16. Pascal, ***Pascal's Pensées,*** p. 78.
17. Quaker Hill Conference Center, ***Friends Consultation,*** address by Jan Wood, p. 12.
18. Green, p. 66. Compare Burtness, p. 71: ". . . every facet of life exists in the context of fundamental ambiguity."
19. Dunne, p. 39. A century earlier, John Henry Newman used a similar metaphor:

 Lead, kindly Light, amid the encircling gloom,
 Lead thou me on;
 The night is dark, and I am far from home,
 Lead thou me on;
 Keep thou my feet: I do not ask to see
 The distant scene; one step enough for me . . .

Newman, "Lead, Kindly Light," pp. 74f. Many hymnals contain this poem in the form of a hymn. See, for example, ***Hymnal 1940,*** Hymn 430.

20. Green, p. 96.
21. Called to resist the evil of Nazi Germany, Bonhoeffer wrote, "God . . . demands responsible action in a bold venture of faith and promises forgiveness and consolation to the person who becomes a sinner in that venture." ***Letters and Papers,*** p. 6.

Chapter 4. What Conditions Help Discern God's Call?

1. Compare Green, p. 55f, "The Climate of Discernment." Green (pp. 58–61) says three qualities are necessary to discern God's call: desire to do God's will, openness to God, and knowledge of God.
2. Green, p. 55, argues that some conditions are "necessary" before a person can even begin to discern, because discernment requires the same "total commitment to the Lord" as Jesus had in relation to his Father. Yet stating that a person must always meet certain conditions and have a total commitment to the Lord in order to discern God's call seems to limit God's power. With God's grace, even the spiritually diffident may come to hear and recognize the Lord's voice and follow where it leads. With God, "all things are possible" (Mark 10:27). Consequently, while it is fair to say that having some qualities or predispositions for discernment is ***helpful,*** to say that they are "necessary" may underestimate God. To disqualify ourselves because we do not have specific qualities could cause us to bury our

talents in fear rather than risk response to God who calls us. Compare Matt. 25:25.

3. Orsy, pp. 160–61.
4. Orsy, p. 158. See Toner, p. 126: "It is a presumption that any group of relatively good Christians can at the drop of the hat enter on discernment of God's will and do it with a few prayers and a lot of hot debate. . . ."
5. This is not to say that trust in the Lord is easily achieved. Kelsey tells the story of a traveler who came to the edge of a chasm which he could not cross. Suddenly, a tightrope appeared and, on it, an acrobat pushing a wheelbarrow with another man inside. When they reached the side where the traveler was standing, the acrobat asked the traveler, "Don't you think I can do it again?" The traveler replied, "Why, yes. I certainly believe you can." The performer asked again. When the answer was the same, he pointed to the wheelbarrow and said, "Good! Then get in and I will take you across." (***The Other Side of Silence***, p. 41.)

   For some people, trust comes over time and through experience as they grow in confidence that all things work to the good for those who love God. One aspect of trusting God may be recollecting our past and, in a sense, "forgiving God" for what has gone before. Dunne, p. 58, suggests that a person can suffer all through life from resentment at one's fate and that forgiving God may be "the only way to abolish the hell of this resentment." To make peace with God for the past opens the path of trust in God for the future.
6. See Toner, p. 127.

7. Numerous writers have emphasized the importance of openness in discernment. Ignatius's now-classic description (p. 85) is of an "indifference" to all but God's will:

   > . . . I must remain indifferent and free from any inordinate attachments so that I am not more inclined or disposed [one way or the other]. I must rather be like the equalized scales of balance, ready to follow the course which . . . is more for the glory and praise of God . . .

   This concept has come to be known as "Ignatian indifference."
8. de Waal, p. 43.
9. Green, p. 59. See Toner, p. 129: "Consciously admitted ignorance about the right answer to the question at issue is the only valid starting point for discernment."
10. de Waal, pp. 42, 153. The idea of listening with our bodies may be unfamiliar to some, but it is not difficult to understand. For example, if our bodies tell us that we are tired, it may be a sign that we are doing too much. Sanford writes, "Very often . . . our body is telling us something because we have not been open to hearing it in any other way" ***(Healing and Wholeness,*** p. 31).
11. de Waal, p. 43.
12. Authors' (free) translation.
13. de Waal, p. 153.
14. See Teresa of Avila, ***Interior Castle,*** p. 39.
15. Compare Green, p. 66; Teresa of Avila, ***Interior Castle,*** pp. 37–39.
16. See ***Cloud of Unknowing,*** chapters 13 and 14, discussing humility, perfect and imperfect.

17. Compare de Waal, pp. 43, 146; Green, pp. 11–13.
18. Compare Kelsey, ***The Other Side of Silence,*** pp. 22–23, discussing the various personality types developed by C.J. Jung and their relationship to spiritual development. Among other things, Kelsey suggests that extroverts—persons who find energy and meaning in contact with others—will likely find their prayer life geared to service to others. While this does not mean that extroverts do not need time for quiet and reflection, it may mean that finding such time requires special effort. For a more extended discussion of the relationship between personality type and spiritual life, see Michael and Norrisey.
19. Lewis, ***The Screwtape Letters,*** p. 49.
20. Bonhoeffer, ***Letters and Papers,*** p. 169.
21. Quaker Hill Conference Center, ***Friends Consultation,*** address by Jan Wood, p. 15.
22. Ibid.
23. Ibid.
24. Lewis, ***The Screwtape Letters,*** p. 132.
25. de Waal, p. 46.
26. Fox, p. 54.
27. Kelsey, ***Discernment: A Study in Ecstasy and Evil,*** p. 83, distinguishes a person who speaks with authority from a person who thinks he or she has a full grasp of the truth.
28. Compare Dunne, p. 42, discussing the "self-defeating" quality of the pursuit of certainty: the more a person seeks certainty, the more uncertain the person becomes.

Chapter 5. Is It God We Are Hearing?

1. de Waal, p. 105. Compare Teresa of Avila, ***Interior Castle,*** p. 232:

   > . . . the devil sometimes puts ambitious desires into our hearts, so that, instead of setting our hand to the work which lies nearest to us, and thus serving Our Lord in ways within our power, we may rest content with having desired the impossible.

2. Compare L'Engle, p. 140:

   > But neither was Jesus adequate to the situation. He did not feed all the poor, only a few. He did not heal all the lepers, or give sight to all the blind, or drive out all the unclean spirits. Satan wanted him to do all this, but he didn't.

3. de Waal, p. 73.
4. Teilhard de Chardin, ***Building the Earth,*** p. 76: ". . . the perfection and usefulness of each nucleus of human energy in relation to the whole depend in the last resort upon whatever is unique and incommunicable in each of them."
5. Quaker Hill Conference Center, ***Consultation of Friends,*** Howard R. Macy, "Discerning Gifts in Ministry," p. 3: "[G]ifts in ministry may or may not coincide with apparent natural abilities, interests or training."
6. Hammarskjöld, p. 120. Compare Mark 10:27: "With God, all things are possible."

7. God may have many reasons for calling a person to service outside the person's normal skills. For example, a person who is an accountant may constantly be asked to serve on finance committees. Yet God may call the accountant to travel a new road—to act in a play, to take communion to the sick, to work at a shelter—in order to open new doors and bring new growth in the Spirit.

   Serving God in an unfamiliar capacity can evoke humility. A talented person who undertakes a task and succeeds may be tempted to take credit for the result; a less-gifted person who undertakes the same task successfully is more likely to see God's hand in it.
8. Compare John of the Cross, p. 606: "If the Spirit of Him who has power descends upon you, do not abandon your place," quoting from Eccles. 10:4.
9. de Waal, p. 62.
10. de Waal, p. 70.
11. John of the Cross, "The Ascent of Mount Carmel" and "Dark Night of the Soul."
12. For insight into the deficiencies of spiritual directors, see John of the Cross, pp. 626–34.
13. Johnston, p. 116. See also Fenhagen, ***Holiness,*** p. 45: "The commandments of God have too often been presented in our tradition only as moral precepts by which we can judge our neighbors, rather than as a vision in which the call to holiness is rooted. Our concern is not to have presented to us a blueprint for life that will allow us to avoid risk, but rather a vision of integrity from which decisions are made and life is lived."
14. Compare Brown, **Churches,** pp. 133–34. Brown cites Jesus' willingness to pay the temple tax despite having no obligation to do so as an example of

refraining from asserting a principle in order to avoid giving offense (Matt. 17:24–27). He suggests that a willingness to forgo insistence on a principle is especially important where a threat or challenge to personal prestige may be involved. The same reasoning can be applied to moral principles, especially where, on reflection, pastoral concerns outweigh the principle advanced.

15. God's call transcends moral rules. See, for example, Kierkegaard, ***Fear and Trembling,*** p. 77, reflecting on the paradox of God's apparently calling Abraham to murder his son, Isaac. Unless Abraham, acting on faith, silenced or disobeyed the moral rule against murder—in what Kierkegaard (p. 77) calls "a teleological suspension of the ethical"—he could not have heard or obeyed God's call to obedience.

    Compare St. Paul's discussion of how faith in God replaces the law:

    > Before this faith came, we were close prisoners in the custody of law, pending the revelation of faith. The law was thus put in charge of us until Christ should come, when we should be justified through faith; and now that faith has come, its charge is at an end. (Gal. 3:23–25, NEB)

    More recently, theologians have discussed the inability of moral rules to address the facts and circumstances of situations in which we need to listen for God's call. See, for example, Burtness, p. 54: "Ethical 'principles' miscarry. They are not after all able to master reality at the decisive moment."

16. Compare Ignatius of Loyola, p. 85. The fourth point in Ignatius' first method of making a wise and good

choice is to examine the advantages and disadvantages of a proposed action and, alternatively, the advantages and disadvantages of not taking the action.

17. Futrell, ***Ignatian Discernment,*** p. 81.
18. Compare Green, p. 31. Green states that God is faithful and cannot contradict God's self. This is helpful to consider in situations where we are receiving seemingly conflicting messages about a call. The danger in using consistency as a guideline for discernment is that we may end up ascribing our human, limited view of consistency to what God is doing. God's purpose for us can be like a shoot emerging from the ground in early spring. The shoot does not resemble the daffodil it will one day become; it is not, in form, texture, or quality, the same as the flower. Yet, in unity of growth, it brings forth the flower. By imposing our own external sense of unity and spiritual growth on God, we may miss a flowering of God's call simply because we view it as inconsistent with the stalk that has come before.

    Nevertheless, God may be telling us something through the apparently conflicting evidence. If we take time to ponder the possibilities, we may be led to new insights.
19. McNeill, Morrisson, and Nouwen, throughout. Compare Fox, p. 121: "The poor are all too often left to God. Therefore, forget those who are better placed and remember the poor."
20. Compare Teresa of Avila, ***Life,*** p. 239.
21. Compare Brown, **Churches,** p. 44.
22. Ibid., p. 150.
23. Ibid., p. 113. In another book, ***Crucified Christ,*** Brown gives an example of the need to consider the

context of Scriptural writings. In ***Crucified Christ,*** he notes (pp. 15, 62–63) that the passion narratives of Matthew and John were written at the end of the first century, a time of tremendous hostility between early Christians and Jews. He urges all who preach during Holy Week to clearly inform congregations of the context of these passion accounts so that their implicit message of anti-Semitism does not go unexplained. Brown writes (p. 16):

> Sooner or later Christian believers must wrestle with the limitations imposed on the Scriptures by the circumstances in which they were written. They must be brought to see that some attitudes found in the Scriptures, however explicable in the times in which they originated, may be wrong attitudes if repeated today. They must reckon with the implications inherent in the fact that God has revealed ***in words of men.*** [Emphasis in original]

24. Brown, ***Churches,*** pp. 40–41.
25. Ibid., p. 108.
26. Ibid., p. 88 n. 128. Compare John 13:3–5.
27. Compare Fox, p. 61, quoting Meister Eckhart's view that loving God for the sake of outward riches or inward consolation is no different from loving a cow for its milk, cheese, and profit—such love is not for God but is for one's own advantage.
28. Green, p. 171, quoting Julian of Norwich. See Futrell, p. 63; Teresa of Avila, ***Interior Castle,*** p. 91.
29. Compare Ignatius of Loyola, p. 133. See Green, pp. 168–71.

30. Teresa of Avila, ***Interior Castle,*** p. 168. Compare Lewis, ***Surprised by Joy,*** p. 18: ". . . joy is never in our power."
31. See Teresa of Avila, ***Interior Castle,*** p. 188. Although Teresa is treating the subject of visions, a temporary experience of disorientation followed by calm and serenity can accompany other spiritual experiences. Commotion arises because what had served as an apparently satisfactory understanding of matters is being pulled out from under us. Peace follows as a new understanding (founded on a sounder comprehension of reality) emerges to replace the old.
32. Teresa of Avila, ***Interior Castle,*** p. 167.
33. Futrell, ***Ignatian Discernment,*** p. 57. "Felt-knowledge" translates the Ignatian concept, ***sentir,*** which describes the interaction of feelings and thoughts that confirm or question a call. Futrell, p. 56, writes, "It is through attention to one's ***sentir,*** the vital testimony of profound human feelings during the discernment process, that one discovers the ***orientation*** of his impulses towards decision or action," and, at the same time, "the ***origin*** of these impulses" (emphasis in original).
34. Teresa of Avila, ***Interior Castle,*** p. 185.
35. Compare the Ignatian concept of "consolation without previous cause," which refers to an unsought and unexpected spiritual experience. The experience is so clear that, at the time, there is no doubt of God's presence. See Ignatius of Loyola, pp. 133–34; see also Teresa of Avila, ***Interior Castle,*** p. 141.
36. See Teresa of Avila, ***Interior Castle,*** pp. 150–51, 179–80, 185. See also Teresa of Avila, ***Life,*** p. 236:

"... the Lord impresses His words upon the memory so that it is impossible to forget them...."

37. de Waal, p. 137.
38. Compare Ignatius of Loyola, p. 130.
39. In an August 30, 1990, letter, David A. Scott, ethics professor at the Virginia Theological Seminary, expressed his admiration for students who deferred seminary study because of family commitments. Scott is concerned about accepting single parents as students who would spend "even less time than they might with their small children."
40. Conversation, June 5, 1989, with Michael J. Sheeran, S.J., vice president of academic affairs of Regis College in Denver, Colorado, and author of ***Beyond Majority Rule.***
41. Fox, p. 32: "People who dwell in God dwell in the eternal now"; Lewis, ***Mere Christianity,*** pp. 146–47. See generally Tillich, ***The Eternal Now,*** pp. 122–32.
42. Johnston, p. 117.
43. Kelsey, ***Discernment: A Study in Ecstasy and Evil,*** p. 83.
44. See Green, chapters 6 and 7.

Chapter 6. Why Is Community Important in Discerning God's Call?

1. Compare John of the Cross, p. 132: God "draws near to those who come together in an endeavor to know" the truth.
2. Bonhoeffer, ***Letters and Papers,*** pp. 236–37: "I feel that it's one of the laws of spiritual understanding that one's own thoughts, when they are understood by others, at the same time always undergo a trans-

formation and liberation through the medium of the person."

3. John of the Cross, p. 184.
4. See John of the Cross, p. 184. John of the Cross discusses this in relation to a spiritual director, but others trained in the area of discernment can also help a person seeking discernment. Compare Futrell, ***Ignatian Discernment,*** p. 55, discussing Ignatius' emphasis on the need to consult with others in proportion to the complexity of the issue.
5. John of the Cross, p. 182, states that God does not want us to bestow entire credence on his communications, or be confirmed in their strength and security, until they pass through the human channel of the mouth of another person.
6. Woolman, throughout.
7. Ibid.
8. Compare Teilhard de Chardin, ***Building the Earth,*** p. 81, discussing the powers of the universe that "gradually assume the form of a fundamental affinity which links individuals to each other and to their transcendent Center."

Chapter 7. Discerning Call in Community

1. Compare Futrell, ***Communal Discernment,*** p. 177. Paraphrasing Carl Rogers, Futrell writes that one reason people find it so hard to really listen to one another is that when they do, there is always a possibility of having to change—which all of us tend to fear and resist.
2. Tillich, ***Love, Power, and Justice,*** p. 84.

3. See Futrell, ***Communal Discernment,*** p. 173: "The entire process of spiritual discernment is prayer. Consequently, it is vital to establish an atmosphere of prayer, of openness to the Holy Spirit and to one another." See also Futrell, ***Ignatian Discernment,*** p. 72: "Failure in communal discernment most often is the result of the fact that the [persons] engaging in the discernment do not pray. It is as simple—and as difficult—as that."
4. Bonhoeffer, ***Life Together,*** p. 79.
5. Bonhoeffer, ***Life Together,*** p. 80. While Scripture, intuition, and experience have taught Christians the value of silence, experiments in education document the salutary effects of increased silence, or "wait time," in a classroom. See Rowe; Swift and Gooding; and Tobin. Wait time refers to (1) deliberately increased amounts of time a teacher allows between asking a question and expecting a response, and (2) deliberately extended lengths of time a teacher permits a student to pause when responding to a question before determining that the student has finished. These experiments show that as the pace of interchange in a classroom slows down, the quality of the teacher's questions increases; the quality of the students' participation goes up; the level of thinking in the class rises; the number of students taking part in class discussion increases; the way students listen to each other improves; and discipline problems decrease.
6. ***Consensus*** means the sense of the group. ***Sense of the meeting*** is a Quaker term that has a spiritual connotation suggesting a settled place to which the Holy Spirit has led the group; it is sought through silence and listening together, unhampered by preconceived

opinions. ***Unity*** and ***concord*** are other terms that Quakers sometimes use interchangeably with ***sense of the meeting***.

7. For a fuller discussion of spiritual consensus, see Farnham, Hull, and McLean, chapter 6.

Chapter 8. Support for Ministries

1. In a letter of November 5, 1990, James Fenhagen, dean of the General Theological Seminary, went so far as to say, "Never call someone for ministry until a system of support has been established."

Epilogue

1. Rilke, pp. 34–35.

Appendix 2. Types of Questions to Raise When Serving in Discernment Groups

1. Merton, ***The Seven Storey Mountain,*** pp. 139–40.

Annotated Bibliography

Unless otherwise noted, Scripture quotations are from the New Revised Standard Version Bible. Other versions are indicated throughout book by the following abbreviations:

JB: Jerusalem Bible
KJV: King James Version
NIV: New International Version
REB: Revised English Bible
TNIV: Today's New International Version

Bacon, Margaret Hope. ***Mothers of Feminism: The Story of Quaker Women in America.*** New York: Harper & Row, 1986.

This book shows how a handful of dedicated people living out their sense of call exerted influence far greater than their numbers. These Quaker women serve as an inspiration, reminding us that we can have an important impact when we act from our Christian conviction. Historical and fascinating.

Bacovin, Helen, trans. ***The Way of a Pilgrim.*** Garden City, NY: Doubleday, 1978.

The story of a Russian peasant who, upon hearing the exhortation in Paul's First Letter to the Thessalonians to "pray constantly," is filled with a deep desire to know what this means. Of this desire he is told, "Recognize in this a call from God and be at peace." He learns the Jesus prayer, "Lord Jesus Christ, have mercy on me," and travels his entire life from place to place, saying the prayer with lips and heart, sharing the prayer with others.

Barclay, William. A translation of ***The Gospel of Matthew*** with an introduction and interpretation, vol. 2 (chaps. 11 to 28). Revised edition. ***The Daily Study Bible Series.*** Philadelphia: Westminister Press, 1975.

Benedict. ***The Rule of St. Benedict.*** Translated by Anthony C. Meisel and M. L. del Mastro. Garden City, NY: Doubleday, 1975.

Discusses persuasively the importance of meeting in community to consider significant matters and of providing support for one another's work. Also points out the value of hearing from the least seasoned members of the community as well as the contribution of a balanced and well-ordered life.

Bonhoeffer, Dietrich.

Bonhoeffer's theology, written in the cauldron that was Nazi Germany of the 1930s and 1940s, has continued to inspire, shape, and direct Christian concern and action for social and international justice ever since.

Letters and Papers from Prison. Edited by Eberhard Bethge. New York: Macmillan, 1979.

Confronts us with God's call to assume a share of responsibility for the course of history.

Life Together. Translated by John W. Doberstein. New York: Harper & Row, 1954.

Defines Christianity as community through and in Jesus Christ. Useful discussions are found on the importance and use of silence, the value and content of meditation, and the ministry of listening.

The Cost of Discipleship. Revised edition. Translated by R. H. Fuller, with some revision by Irmgard Booth. New York: Macmillan, 1963.

Focuses on Jesus and his call to us to be disciples. "What is his will for us today?" Bonhoeffer asks, "What [is it] Jesus Christ himself wants us to do?" And, he asks, "if we answer the call to discipleship, where will it lead us? What decisions and partings will it demand?" This book is important for anyone seeking to respond to God's call.

The Book of Common Prayer. New York: Church Publishing, 1979.

Brown, Raymond E. ***The Churches the Apostles Left Behind.*** New York: Paulist, 1984.

Brown's scholarly grasp of Scripture and of life in the apostolic era is unparalleled. This book is an important resource on Scripture and Christian community.

A Crucified Christ in Holy Week: Essays on the Four Gospel Passion Narratives. Collegeville, MN: Liturgical Press, 1986.

Meditations on the differing accounts of Jesus' suffering and death. Helpful discussion of the context in which Scripture was written. Excellent Lenten reading.

Brown, Raymond E., and John P. Meier. ***Antioch and Rome: New Testament Cradles of Catholic Christianity.*** New York: Paulist, 1983.

This exploration of diversity and dissension in the early church provides guidance for those trying to discern God's call in circumstances of conflict.

Buber, Martin. ***The Writings of Martin Buber.*** Cleveland: World, 1969.

Burtness, James H. ***Shaping the Future: The Ethics of Dietrich Bonhoeffer.*** Philadelphia: Fortress, 1985.

A wealth of important material. The thesis: life is always filled with ambiguity, but we need to assume responsibility. We need to take action after earnestly looking at our situation at a given time and place, considering the consequences of action or lack of it, examining our hearts, and giving due weight to the reality of God and the world together in Christ.

The Cloud of Unknowing and ***The Book of Privy Counseling.*** Edited by William Johnston. Garden City, NY: Doubleday, 1973.

Written by an anonymous English mystic of the fourteenth century, these two works address the person who feels drawn to contemplative prayer. They contain invaluable guidance for anyone trying to discern a call to contemplation.

Cobb, John. ***God and the World.*** Philadelphia: Westminister Press, 1969.

Curry, Michael B. ***Crazy Christians: A Call to Follow Jesus.*** New York: Morehouse Publishing, 2013.

This wonderfully readable book overflows with insight about how God works in us and through us. For example, it shows that what can seem like a call to address a specific personal situation might have an ultimate purpose that goes beyond anything we can imagine. It warns that a true call may well be countercultural and can involve considerable risk. Warm and down-to-earth.

de Waal, Esther. ***Seeking God: The Way of St. Benedict.*** Collegeville, MN: Liturgical Press, 1984.

Esther de Waal is an English historian whose extraordinary insight into the Rule of St. Benedict brings Benedictine principles of spirituality alive to ordinary people for their daily life. This book is filled with wisdom that is valuable in discernment.

Delio, Ilia. ***The Unbearable Wholeness of Being: God, Evolution, and the Power of Love.*** Maryknoll, NY: Orbis, 2013.

This book is an amazing exposition of the work of Teilhard de Chardin. Exploring his mystical theology in light of scientific advances of the late twentieth and early twenty-first centuries, Delio elucidates the evolution of spirituality in relation to the evolution of the cosmos, which began at the moment of the Big Bang—with the unifying power of love energy at its very core. Here on earth an ever forward moving process is in progress that brings experience, judgment, reflection, creative thinking, and fragments of thought together in a way that reveals truth, creates knowledge, and leads to wholeness. Delio envisions a time when the major world religions converge as they focus on the universal beliefs that are at the heart of their faith. This is not to suggest that they abandon what is unique to their heritage. It does imply that they will bond at a deep level, connected by the love energy that flows through them. The book is a heavy read filled with profound insights. Hearty nourishment for the searching soul.

Diocese of Bethlehem (Pennsylvania) of the Episcopal Church. ***The Manual of Policies, Guidelines, and Requirements for Seeking the Ordained Ministry.*** Accompanied by "Additional Guidelines for the Parish Discernment Fellowship." Bethlehem, PA: Diocese of Bethlehem, 1984.

Dougherty, Rose Mary. ***Discernment: A Path to Spiritual Awakening.*** Mahwah, NJ: Paulist Press, 2009.

This little book (80 pages in total) offers a clear and succinct guide to the essentials of discernment for spiritual seekers of all types. The author, a Roman Catholic nun, has led retreats and workshops, and offered spiritual direction to inquirers, for over three decades. She also teaches Zen to people wishing to integrate contemplative presence and just action in their lives. This is an excellent guide to those new to discernment and a helpful refresher for more experienced practitioners.

Dunne, John S. ***The Way of All the Earth: Experiments in Truth and Religion.*** Notre Dame, IN: University of Notre Dame Press, 1972.

An original thinker gathers insights offered by other religions and applies them to the Christian journey with God. Rich in descriptions to help us see our lives as spiritual adventures with God as our companion.

Eliot, T.S. ***Four Quartets.*** New York: Harcourt Brace Jovanovich, 1971.

A small book of poems exploring remembered experience in life's pilgrimage toward God.

Farnham, Suzanne G., and Timothy H. Grayson. ***Keeping in Tune with God.*** New York: Church Publishing, 2011. Available for free digital download at www.listeninghearts.org.

An essential resource for clergy and the people who love, work with, and care about them, *Keeping in Tune with God* directly addresses clergy hunger to stay connected to vocation, to God, and to community. Based on the tested wisdom of Listening Hearts discernment, the book provides clergy with encouraging words and practices to develop their relationships with God, their families, and friends; to carry the practice of spiritual discernment into the life of their congregations; and to work more effectively with other leaders to nurture the life of Christ in the world around them.

Farnham, Suzanne G., Stephanie A. Hull, and R. Taylor McLean. ***Grounded in God: Listening Hearts Discernment for Group Deliberations.*** Harrisburg, PA: Morehouse Publishing, 1996.

Explains spiritual discernment as it relates to seeking God's guidance for group decision-making. Appendices provide step-by-step suggestions for implementing the ideas presented.

Fenhagen, James C. ***Invitation to Holiness.*** Harrisburg, PA: Morehouse Publishing, 1991.

Here we find the disturbing thought that Christians are called not to virtue but to service in and for the world in companionship with each other and the Lord. A section on spiritual direction is helpful for those not familiar with the term. Sections on vocation, the importance of framing and considering questions without insisting on immediate answers, and the purpose of the worshiping community are also of special relevance to those committed to discerning God's call in community.

Mutual Ministry: New Vitality for the Local Church. New York: Seabury, 1977.

This down-to-earth book helps prepare a foundation for mutual ministry in the parish.

Fox, Matthew. ***Meditations with Meister Eckhart.*** Santa Fe, NM: Bear & Company, 1983.

Futrell, John Carroll. ***Ignatian Discernment.*** Vol. 2, no. 2 of ***Studies in the Spirituality of Jesuits.*** St. Louis, MO: American Assistancy Seminar on Jesuit Spirituality, 1969.

A primer for understanding the language and meaning of the "Rules for the Discernment of Spirits" section of ***The Spiritual Exercises of Ignatius.*** The paper strives to teach how to apply

Ignatian concepts of discernment to situations of everyday life.

Futrell. ***Communal Discernment: Reflections on Experience.*** Vol. 4, no. 5 of ***Studies in the Spirituality of Jesuits.*** St. Louis, MO: American Assistancy Seminar on Jesuit Spirituality, 1972.

Applies Ignatian concepts of discernment to communities seeking discernment of God's call to the community.

Green, Thomas H. ***Weeds among the Wheat: Where Prayer and Action Meet.*** Notre Dame, IN: Ave Maria Press, 1984.

This work by a Jesuit provides an excellent synthesis of Ignatian discernment with a good bit of Carmelite spirituality sprinkled in.

Hammerskjöld, Dag. ***Markings.*** Translated by Leif Sjoberg and W. H. Auden. New York: Knopf, 1964.

This spiritual diary of the former secretary general of the United Nations is a good resource for reflective prayer.

Heron, Alastair. ***Gifts and Ministries: A Discussion Paper on Eldership.*** London: Quaker Home Service, 1987.

This paper about an issue close to the Quaker community offers valuable insight into questions of mutual responsibility that arise in any Christian community.

Holl, Karl. "The History of the Word Vocation ***(Beruf).***" Translated by Herber F. Peacock. Baltimore, MD: Listening Hearts Ministries, unpublished paper.

The Hymnal of the Protestant Episcopal Church in the United States of America: 1940. New York: Church Pension Fund, 1940.

Ignatius of Loyola. ***The Spiritual Exercises of St. Ignatius.*** Translated by Anthony Mottola. Garden City, NY: Doubleday, 1964.

This classic, highly intellectual work of spirituality contains Ignatius' chief work on discernment, "Rules for the Discernment of Spirits." Related chapters include "Introduction to Making a Choice of a Way of Life."

John of the Cross. ***The Collected Works of John the Cross.*** Translated by Kieran Kavanaugh, O.C.D., and Otilio Rodriguez, O.C.D. Washington, DC: Institute of Carmelite Studies Publications, 1976.

The author, a sixteenth-century mystic and cofounder of the Discalced Carmelites, speaks to the Christian who has a disciplined prayer life and a bent for contemplative prayer. Those with inadequate background risk the danger of misconstruing what he says. The first two books in this volume, ***The Ascent of Mount Carmel*** and ***The Dark Night,*** are gold mines of insight on discernment. They combine to form one work expounding upon his poem, "The Dark Night," one of the finest poems of Spanish literature.

The Living Flame of Love, another book in the collection, speaks especially to one seeking discernment in a period of intense spiritual transformation.

Johnston, William. ***The Still Point: Reflections on Zen and Christian Mysticism.*** New York: Fordham University Press, 1970.

The Zen perspective explored in this work can help the Christian prepare to approach discernment with heart and mind unencumbered.

Julian of Norwich. ***Revelations of Divine Love.*** Translated into modern English by Clifton Wolters. Harmondsworth, England: Penguin, 1966.

These meditations on visions of God show an entire life enfolded in God's love.

Jung, Carl G. "Psychotherapists or the Clergy." In ***Psychology and Religion: West and East.*** Translated by R. F. C. Hull. Princeton, NJ: Princeton University Press, 1969.

Kelsey, Morton. ***Discernment: A Study in Ecstasy and Evil.*** New York: Paulist, 1978.

The Other Side of Silence. Paramus, NJ: Paulist Press, 1976.

A practical guide to Christian meditation that includes discussion on practicing silence and using images.

Kierkegaard, Søren. ***A Kierkegaard Anthology.*** Edited by Robert Bretail. Princeton, NJ: Princeton University Press, 1946.

Fear and Trembling with ***Sickness Unto Death.*** Princeton, NJ: Princeton University Press, 1954.

Lawrence, Brother [Nicolas Herman, 1611–91]. ***The Practice of the Presence of God.*** Cincinnati: Forward Movement Publications.

The spirit of a Carmelite kitchen brother of the seventeenth century who lived his life as prayer, emanates from the pages of this short book. Ultimately, discernment depends on a close personal relationship with God; this book helps to lay the groundwork for that to develop.

L'Engle, Madeleine. ***The Irrational Season.*** San Francisco: Harper & Row, 1977.

Lewis, C.S. ***The Great Divorce.*** New York: Macmillan, 1946.

Herein lie some pithy insights of value in discernment.

Mere Christianity. New York: Collier Books, Macmillan, 1952.

The author's classic defense of Christianity. In a short section "Beyond Personality," Lewis provides perspective on the human concept of time, which has relevance for discernment.

The Screwtape Letters: How a Senior Devil Instructs a Junior Devil in the Art of Temptation. New York: Macmillan, 1961.

Lewis's great ironic work on how good and evil operate in the world and on how to distinguish between them.

Surprised by Joy. New York: Harcourt Brace Jovanovich, 1955.

Luther, Martin. ***Martin Luther: Selections from His Writings.*** Edited by John Dillenberger. Garden City, NY: Anchor, 1961.

May, Gerald G. ***Addiction and Grace.*** San Francisco: Harper & Row, 1988.

A new way of looking at what classical spirituality calls "detachment."

McNeill, Donald P., Douglas A. Morrison, and Henri J. M. Nouwen. ***Compassion: A Reflection on the Christian Life.*** Garden City, NY: Doubleday, 1982.

Helpful discussions on obedience, on the distinction between vocation and career, and on community as it relates to ministry make this a good book on servanthood.

Merton, Thomas. ***New Seeds of Contemplation.*** New York: New Directions, 1972.

One of Merton's most widely read works, this book offers profound reflections on humility, obedience, detachment, personal identity, and contemplative experience.

The Seven Storey Mountain. New York: Harcourt Brace Jovanovich, 1948.

Thoughts in Solitude. New York: Farrar, Straus and Giroux, 1958.

Michael, Chester P., and Marie C. Norrisey. ***Prayer and Temperament: Different Prayer Forms for Different***

Personality Types. Charlottesville, VA. Open Door, 1984.

Explaining the varied spiritual needs of different people, this book explores why what works for one person may not work for the next. Understanding these differences is helpful for discerners.

Nelson-Isaacs, Sky. ***Living in Flow.*** Berkeley, CA: North Atlantic Books, 2019.

In this readable, first-person account, this book engages the reader in understanding how our choices shape the world we experience through meaningful coincidences. The author's light, humble touch makes the read worthwhile.

Newman, John Henry. ***A Newman Reader.*** Edited by Francis X. Connelly. Garden City, NY: Doubleday, 1964.

Nouwen, Henri, with Michael Christensen and Rebecca Laird. ***Discernment: Reading the Signs of Daily Life.*** New York: Harper Collins, 2015.

Twenty-five years after his death, Henri Nouwen remains possibly the most widely read and authoritative spiritual guide of our time, and for good reason. He writes in an engaging and personal style that speaks to everyone who yearns for a closer relationship with God, regardless of where they are on their spiritual journey. This book was drawn from original materials found in the Henri J. M. Nouwen Archives in the Kelly Library at the University of Toronto, and is organized in a way that enables it to be read sequentially by chapter or dipped into at random to be rewarded with a burst of spiritual insight. Each chapter ends with exercises for deeper discernment.

O'Conner, Elizabeth. ***Journey Inward, Journey Outward.*** San Francisco: Harper & Row, 1968.

Orsy, Ladislas. ***Toward a Theological Evaluation of Communal Discernment.*** Vol. 5, no. 5 of ***Studies in the Spirituality of Jesuits.*** St. Louis, MO: American Assistancy Seminar on Jesuit Spirituality, 1972.

Palmer, Parker J. ***A Place Called Community.*** Pendle Hill Pamphlet 212. Wallingford, PA: Pendle Hill, 1977.

Recommended reading on community.

A Hidden Wholeness: The Journey Toward an Undivided Life. San Francisco, John Wiley & Sons, 2004.

Filled with profound insights and practical wisdom applicable to Listening Hearts discernment groups, this work is a solid resource for anyone interested in spiritual discernment.

Let Your Life Speak: Listening for the Voice of Vocation. San Francisco, John Wiley & Sons, 2000.

This book is laced with reflections relevant to finding one's true self.

The Promise of Paradox: A Celebration of Contradictions in the Christian Life. Introduction by Henri Nouwen. San Francisco, John Wiley & Sons, 2008.

The first three chapters of this work shed light on the value of holding apparently opposite truths in creative tension until a larger truth emerges.

Pascal, Blaise. ***Pascal's Pensees,*** trans. by W. F. Trotter. New York: E.P. Dutton & Co., 1958.

Phillips, Jan. ***No Ordinary Time: A Rise of Spiritual and Evolutionary Creativity.*** San Diego: Loving-kindness Foundation, 2011.

This book issues a clarion call to become your true self—the person you were born to be. It encourages the reader to learn through experience what spiritual practices work for them and what spiritual teachings ring true. The author grew up a strong traditional Roman Catholic. As an adult she branched out to explore other faith traditions. She has expanded her understanding of creation by pondering the implications of modern science. She integrates art, music, and creative writing into her faith journey. Undergirding the entire text is an understanding that everything that is, has been, or ever will be in creation is interconnected. The book is a treasure trove of spiritual insights and quotable quotes.

Polanyi, Michael. ***Personal Knowledge.*** New York: Harper & Row, 1964.

Pronzato, Allessandro. ***Meditations on the Sand.*** Translated by Thomas Kala. New York: Alba House, 1983.

A reflective look at our concept of time and the way we relate to our culture and material possessions.

Quaker Hill Conference Center. ***Consultation of Friends on Ministry: Discerning, Nurturing, Recording and Releasing.*** Richmond, IN: Quaker Hill Conference Center, 1981.

Friends Consultation on Discernment. Richmond, IN: Quaker Hill Conference Center, 1985.

Papers by Quaker writers on discernment. Of these, Jan Woods "Spiritual Discernment: The Personal Dimension" is singularly inspiring, a work of poetic prose describing some of the characteristics of a life discerned in God.

Friends Consultation on Spiritual Authority and Accountability. Richmond, IN: Quaker Hill Conference Center, 1984.

An excellent resource on the relationship between authority and accountability.

Rilke, Rainer Maria. ***Letters to a Young Poet.*** Translated by Stephen Mitchell. New York: Random House, 1984.

Rohr, Richard, Daily Meditations, meditations@cac.org, Center for Action and Contemplation. Albuquerque, NM.

Founded by Franciscan priest Richard Rohr, the Center for Action and Contemplation e-mails a free daily meditation to subscribers drawn from the prolific works of Richard Rohr and other contributors to the programs hosted by the center. Rohr has become known throughout the world as an insightful and accessible commentator on religion and spirituality through his numerous books, workshops, conferences, and online materials. His daily meditations and in-person and online programs are a gift to anyone who wants to learn more about the generous heart of God in all its fullness.

Rohr, Richard. ***The Naked Now***. New York: The Crossroad Publishing Company, 2009.

Although discernment is not an explicit topic, this book leaves no doubt that it is the Lord's direction, not his acquiescence, we are seeking. For instance, Rohr's words on spirituality apply with equal force to discernment: "The core task of all good spirituality [discernment] is to teach us to 'cooperate' with what God already wants to do. . . . We are always and forever merely seconding the motion" (p. 23). The same applies to his words on prayer: ". . . true prayer [discernment] stops defending or promoting its ideas and feelings, lets go of any antagonistic attitudes or fears, and waits for, expects, and receives guidance from Another" (p. 102). There are also many other expressions throughout the book that provide insight and guidance for those who are seeking to be listening hearts, grounded in God.

Rovelli, Carl. ***Seven Brief Lessons on Physics***. New York: Riverhead Books, 2016.

As brief as its title, this book describes the mysterious architecture of the universe and the continuous interaction of space and matter, raising the idea that "reality is only interaction."

Rowe, Mary Budd. ***Teaching Science as Continuous Inquiry.*** New York: McGraw-Hill, 1973.

Salinger, J.D. ***Franny and Zooey.*** New York: Bantam Books, 1964.

Sanford, John. ***Dreams: God's Forgotten Language.*** San Francisco: Harper & Row, 1989.

An Episcopal priest who is a Jungian analyst writes about the use of dreams in the Christian spiritual life. Although discerners do not necessarily use dreams in conjunction with their prayer life, it is important that they be able to listen receptively to those who do.

Healing and Wholeness. New York: Paulist, 1977.

Explores the relationship between our health and our life in God.

Schroeder, Gerald L. ***God According to God.*** New York: HarperCollins Publishers, 2009.

In this thought-provoking work, an MIT-trained scientist explores creation and the "free will" of individual quanta with God's desire for a relationship with each of us as told in Hebrew Scripture, also describing the unique place of the planet earth in the universe. Insightful and engaging.

Sedgwick, Timothy F. "Making the Connections: Developing the Ministry of the Laity." ***Ministry Development Journal*** (no. 17, 1989): 3–7.

Sheeran, Michael J. ***Beyond Majority Rule: Voteless Decisions in the Religious Society of Friends.*** Philadelphia: Philadelphia Yearly Meeting, 1983.

This book about the Quakers is written by a Jesuit. It is a primary book Quakers suggest for those interested in the Quaker decision-making process. Since procedures for discernment put forth in ***Listening Hearts*** are based on a Quaker model, this book is important background reading for discerners.

Singer, Michael A. ***The Untethered Soul: The Journey Beyond Yourself.*** Oakland, CA: New Harbinger Publications, 2007.

With more than one million copies sold, this book quickly found a receptive audience and ended up as a *New York Times* bestseller. Writing in an easygoing and often quirky style, Singer invites his readers to take an unsparing look inside themselves and determine what issues they need to address to lead a more fulfilling life. Chapter titles such as "Your inner roommate," "The voice inside your head," and "Letting go of false solidity" indicate the author's desire to challenge readers to be honest about where they are stuck spiritually and find the courage and resources to free themselves.

Swift, Nathan J., and C. Thomas Gooding. "Interaction of Wait Time Feedback and Questioning Instruction on Middle School Science Teaching." ***Journal of Research in Science Teaching,*** 20 (no. 8, 1983): 721–30.

Teilhard de Chardin, Pierre. ***Building the Earth.*** Denville, NJ: Dimension Books, 1965.

Compared to his other works, this book is easy to read and contains many of the ideas found in Teilhard's more ponderous ***The Phenomenon of Man.*** His comprehension of the unity of all creation and the interconnectedness of all things is helpful to discerning God's voice.

Teresa of Avila. ***Interior Castle.*** Translated and edited by E. Allison Peers. Garden City, NY: Doubleday, 1961.

In this work, Teresa combines an unpretentious style with profound insight into call and discernment.

The Life of Teresa of Jesus: The Autobiography of St. Teresa of Avila. Translated and edited by E. Allison Peers. Garden City, NY: Doubleday, 1960.

Long and difficult reading, but filled with wisdom of value to the discerner.

Tillich, Paul. ***The Eternal Now.*** New York: Charles Scribner's Sons, 1963.

Of particular import to the discerner is Tillich's exposition on time found in the title chapter, "The Eternal Now."

Love, Power, and Justice. New York: Oxford University Press, 1954.

Evocative. Concise. Meaty. Understanding the relationships among love, power, and justice can be of great importance in discerning God's call.

Tobin, Kenneth. "Effects of Extended Wait Time on Discourse Characteristics and Achievements in Middle School Grades." ***Journal of Research in Science Teaching,*** 21 (no. 8, 1984): 779–91.

Toner, Jules J. ***A Method for Communal Discernment of God's Will.*** Vol. 3, no. 4 of ***Studies in the***

Spirituality of Jesuits. St. Louis, MO: American Assistancy Seminar on Jesuit Spirituality, 1971.

Ulanov, Ann, and Barry Ulanov. ***Primary Speech.*** Atlanta: John Knox Press, 1982.

Vanauken, Sheldon. ***A Severe Mercy.*** San Francisco: Harper & Row, 1977.

Personal letters of advice from C.S. Lewis highlight this autobiographical work, which casts light on the relationship between personal loss and spiritual growth.

Vanier, Jean. ***Community and Growth.*** New York: Paulist, 1979.

Readable and practical, this book reflects true-life experience in responding to call.

Ware, Timothy, ed. ***The Art of Prayer: An Orthodox Anthology.*** London: Faber & Faber, 1966.

This collection of excerpts on the prayer of the heart is from the Orthodox tradition.

Weil, Simone. ***Waiting for God.*** New York: Harper & Row, 1951.

Whitehead, James D., and Evelyn Eaton Whitehead. ***The Emerging Laity: Returning Leadership to the Community of Faith.*** Garden City, NY: Doubleday, 1986.

As a team, the Whiteheads bring a background in theology, psychology, and church history. They make a strong case for shared leadership in the church.

Williams, H.A. ***Some Day I'll Find You.*** London: Mitchell Beazley Condon, 1982.

Woolman, John. ***The Journals and Major Essays of John Woolman.*** Edited by Phillips P. Moulton. Richmond, IN: Friends United Press, 1989. Reprint of Oxford University Press edition, 1971.

If the Quakers have provided a model for discerning God's call in community, John Woolman serves as its personification. One could find no better book than this to tell what discernment in community has meant in the life of a particular person.

Wright, N.T. ***The Challenge of Jesus***. Downers Grove, IL, 1999.

Bishop Wright identifies love as a basic mode of knowing, "with the love of God as the highest and fullest sort of knowing that there is." In place of what Wright refers to as "the hermeneutics of suspicion" that he says characterize the current age, "[w]e need to articulate, for the post-postmodern world, what we might call an epistemology of love." He makes this point with language from the hymn, "Once In Royal David's City": "And our eyes at last shall see him, through his own redeeming love" and closes with his own poem (p. 197):

Let me trust, and see,
And let love's eyes pursue
and set me free.

Glossary

Discernment Terminology

A Glossary by Category

Different strands of spirituality and different people employ different terminology when discussing discernment. In some cases, two or more terms may have essentially the same meaning. In other cases, words may have similar meanings, but with definite distinctions. The list that follows has been assembled to help people navigate readings and discussions that relate to discernment. It is arranged by category so the reader can easily compare terms that are similar or closely related.

Calling

The Spirit of love and truth is continually drawing us to behave in a way that is authentic to the person we are created to be. This applies to the overall direction of our lives as well as to the choices we make as we live life from day to day. In his book ***Let Your Life Speak***, Parker Palmer offers an insightful exploration of this subject based on his own personal pilgrimage.

Call

God continually tries to guide us and communicate with us through the events, situations, and relationships of our life—through our thoughts, feelings, senses, imagination, and intuition. This can be understood as God's voice or God's call.

The heart

The heart in Hebrew-Christian tradition has more than a physical nature. It is seen as the core of the person, in the center of the body, encompassing the mind, soul, and spirit.

Ministry

When we respond to God's call, what we do as a positive response is considered ministry. This includes the way we relate to people at home, in the workplace, in the church, and in the wider community, as well as ways in which we reach out to address the needs of all creation. For some persons, this includes a professional vocation in the church.

The self

Carl Jung referred to the true center of one's being as the self. This is the place within which all aspects of one's being, dark and light, are integrated and in harmony. As a person moves toward the self, one is pursuing God's call.

True self

As one lives in an intimate relationship with God, following where God leads, a person becomes more and more fully one's true self, in effect living in accordance with one's call.

Vocation

Vocation comes from the Latin word that means call and usually refers to the overall focus meant for one's life. Often it is used to refer to the work of an ordained person, but it is by no means limited to those considered "professional" ministers.

Discernment

The verb "to discern" – meaning to sort out, to sift through, to distinguish – is widely used in the secular world as well as in the church. The noun "discernment," however, is used almost exclusively in religious circles, but suggests different things to different groups of people. In order to avoid confusion, it is helpful to specify the type of discernment one is talking about.

Discernment of call

This is an effort to distinguish the voice of God from other voices that tell us what to do, such as the voice of our parents echoing through the years, voices of teachers and mentors who have been important to us, voices of friends, civic leaders, and religious leaders; voices from nature, art, music, literature, and the media. Often God does speak to us through these voices, but not everything they say is God's word for us. And what is God's call in one time and place may not be God's call for us in a similar situation in a different context. Discernment of call involves sorting out the voices.

Discernment of gifts

It is important to know what our gifts are so that we can make conscious use of them and be appropriately thankful. But God often calls us to do things that we do not appear to be qualified to accomplish. In fact, God is inclined to call people to do things for which they seem ill suited. Consider Sarah and Abraham, the childless couple in their old age, being called to become progenitors of an entire race of people. Or Moses, a man with a speech impediment wanted on charges of murder in Egypt, being chosen to go to Pharaoh to plead on behalf of the Hebrews. Throughout the Bible we see examples of people setting out to do what seems impossible, doing so because God has commanded them and they obey. It is only after they step forward in trusting obedience that God gives them what they need to accomplish the task.

Discernment of spirits (*diakrisis pneumaton*)

This is the term that St. Ignatius of Loyola used to connote distinguishing the Spirit of God from other spirits that influence us: the spirit of the times, the spirit of a nation, the spirit of excelling, of winning, of succeeding. Discernment of spirits and discernment of call are essentially the same thing, using a different vocabulary.

Rational discernment in a Christian context

This is the kind of discernment that most Christians use. Typically, it begins and ends with prayers, proceeds with study, discussion, and/or debate, applying Christian principles to arrive at what is essentially a rational decision.

Spiritual discernment

This begins with rational discernment in a Christian context, but goes beyond that to offer ourselves and any preliminary conclusion to God to be taken wherever the Spirit may lead. It involves becoming still, open to God, and not clinging to anything (personal relationships, material possessions, thoughts, feelings, opinions, convictions, or concepts of God) in order to become supple in God's hands and open to the action of the Holy Spirit. It is essentially contemplative prayer, surrendering all to the flow of the Holy Spirit.

People appointed to help a person who seeks God's guidance

Different terms are used by different groups to designate people who assist others in looking for divine guidance. Some traditions use professionals, others use trained non-professionals. Still others require no specific training.

Clearness committee

In most Friends meetings, any member who is wrestling with a concern or issue may request a group to gather with them Quaker style (sitting in stillness, alert to the inner light that burns within each person, speaking only when urged by the Spirit of God, patiently waiting for the light within those present to merge and bring unity) to help develop clarity in handling it. Usually the group consists of between four and six members of the meeting.

Director

Ignatian discernment is guided by a director who is schooled in discernment of spirits based on the teachings of St. Ignatius of Loyola, who founded the Society of Jesus, commonly known as Jesuits.

Discerner

Members of a Listening Hearts discernment group are referred to as discerners.

Discernment group

Some discernment groups are formed to help a particular person with discernment on a continuing and regular basis; such a group is a discernment support group for a particular person. Other groups are formed to meet on a continuing basis to help one another with discernment during regularly scheduled meetings; these are communal discernment support groups. For Listening Hearts discernment, each group is recruited to help a specific person only with a specific issue. The guidelines for a Listening Hearts discernment group are modeled using Parker Palmer's guidelines for a clearness committee. Because the Listening Hearts guidelines do not presuppose familiarity with the culture of the Religious

Society of Friends, they are more extensive and recommend trained discerners. They also incorporate wisdom and experience from other spiritual traditions, especially Ignatian and Carmelite.

Spiritual director

A seasoned person of prayer who accompanies an individual as a guide on his or her spiritual journey. The two usually meet once a month for about an hour, although different arrangements are not uncommon. Many have been trained in formal training programs. Some charge fees; others do not.

A PERSON SEEKING DISCERNMENT

Anyone who yearns to do what God would have him or her do, either in a specific situation or in a more comprehensive sense, is seeking discernment. Those who look for structured help in this quest are sometimes referred to with specific terms.

Focus person

A person who requests a Quaker clearness committee. Listening Hearts has adopted the term to apply to a person who asks for a discernment group.

Seeker

In some Listening Hearts programs, the term seeker is used rather than focus person.

Letting go

Every contemplative spiritual tradition emphasizes the importance of letting go. Clinging to any thought, feeling, person, or thing is an impediment to being fully open to the divine presence.

Detachment

In spiritual theology, this is the term most commonly used for letting go. It implies not being attached to anything, including our concept of God.

Ignatian indifference

This is a term that Jesuits use for detachment.

Signs of God's Spirit

In spiritual discernment, we look for signs of the Spirit to help us sense the strength of God's presence as we seek to align ourselves with God. Should we misinterpret what God is saying to us, we trust that the Holy Spirit will correct our understanding as long as we continue to travel in close communion with God, drawing us back if we get off the right path. Below are some terms that refer to signs that can help us detect God's participation and are specific to a given tradition.

Consolation without previous cause

This is an Ignatian phrase that connotes a spiritual experience that comes to us unsought and unanticipated. It is an experience of the divine presence so vivid that it leaves no doubt that it was God.

Convergence

When a number of things that had no apparent relationship and occurred over an extended period of time suddenly converge and fit together like a puzzle, this is called convergence.

Felt knowledge (*sentir*)

This Ignatian term refers to a dawning of God's call that can come as one pays close attention to thoughts and feelings from one's depths as they interact to reveal the source of one's impulses toward a decision or action.

Leading

A term used by Quakers when referring to a strong spiritual pull to take a particular action.

Persistence

This connotes that the same message keeps coming to a person at different times through unrelated channels. For instance, the message might first come in the course of a conversation with a friend. A few days later, maybe you are watching TV and get the same message. A month later, you hear a song on the radio that carries the message once again. This can be a sign that God is trying to tell you something.

Consensus

Secular consensus suggests sensing together through rational consideration. No votes are taken, but a resolution is arrived at that everyone can accept, which does not imply unanimity. Spiritual discernment awaits a consensus that includes spiritual harmony.

Concord

This word is found in classic Quaker writings and suggests that spiritual oneness has drawn the group together in relation to the matter under consideration.

Sense of the meeting

In a Quaker meeting for business, a sense of the meeting indicates that there is a shared sense that a particular emerging decision is in accordance with God's will. This is articulated by the clerk for approval by the meeting.

Spiritual consensus

This is a consensus that comes when those present have become knit together through the action of the Holy Spirit and everyone present is at peace with the place at which the group has arrived.

Unity

Gathered in silence, Quakers consider a concern before them by practicing reverent speaking and attentive listening until they arrive at an understanding about the matter under consideration in a manner that brings forth spiritual oneness, which they call unity. This is what some call spiritual consensus.

Other resources for people seeking insight and guidance

There are other places to go for help that dovetail with spiritual discernment. They can provide an alternative to spiritual discernment or be used in conjunction with it.

Pastoral counseling

Pastoral counselors help Christians in search of guidance with problems, not avoiding direct questions, often offering observations and insights.

Psychological counseling

Psychological counselors help people explore their inner life in relation to their choices, and tend to delve deeply into past relationships and experiences.

Support group

Some support groups gather on a regular basis to provide encouragement and counsel to a given person. Many support groups are made up of a number of people who share a common situation (parents of young children, adults with aging parents, prostate cancer patients). Such groups meet on a regular basis to encourage one another and discuss the ways they deal with the issues that accompany their circumstances. In some cases, the group is led by a person with expertise in the field that brings them together.

A Prayer of Thomas Merton

God, we have no idea where we are going. We do not see the road ahead of us. We cannot know for certain where it will end. Nor do we really know ourselves, and the fact that we think we are following your will does not mean that we are actually doing so. But we believe that the desire to please you does in fact please you. And we hope we have that desire in all that we are doing. We hope that we will never do anything apart from that desire. And we know that if we do this you will lead us by the right road, though we may know nothing about it. Therefore, we will trust you always though we may seem to be lost and in the shadow of death. We will not fear, for you are ever with us, and you will never leave us to face our perils alone.

Thoughts in Solitude, p. 83, adapted

VISIT THE

LISTENING HEARTS WEBSITE

www.listeninghearts.org

FREE ONLINE RESOURCES

including a library of meditations and a Primer on Spiritual Discernment

PROGRAM POSSIBILITIES

for individuals and groups, as well as training opportunities

PUBLICATIONS

such as our other books, *Grounded in God* and *Keeping in Tune with God*

Facebook.com/ListeningHearts

@GroundedInGod